VAGANOVA TODAY

UNIVERSITY PRESS OF FLORIDA

Florida A&M University, Tallahassee
Florida Atlantic University, Boca Raton
Florida Gulf Coast University, Ft. Myers
Florida International University, Miami
Florida State University, Tallahassee
New College of Florida, Sarasota
University of Central Florida, Orlando
University of Florida, Gainesville
University of North Florida, Jacksonville
University of South Florida, Tampa
University of West Florida, Pensacola

Agrippina Vaganova as a young woman.
Photo: Mariinsky Theatre Archives.

Vaganova Today

The Preservation of Pedagogical Tradition

~

CATHERINE E. PAWLICK

University Press of Florida

Gainesville ~ Tallahassee ~ Tampa ~ Boca Raton

Pensacola ~ Orlando ~ Miami ~ Jacksonville ~ Ft. Myers ~ Sarasota

First cloth printing, 2011
First paperback printing, 2022

27 26 25 24 23 22   6 5 4 3 2 1

LIBRARY OF CONGRESS CATALOGING-IN-PUBLICATION DATA
Pawlick, Catherine E.
Vaganova today : the preservation of pedagogical tradition / Catherine E. Pawlick.
p. cm.
Summary: "An exploration of the continuing influence of the Vaganova Academy
on dancing today"—Provided by publisher.
Includes bibliographical references and index.
ISBN 978-0-8130-3697-7 (hardback) | ISBN 978-0-8130-6871-8 (pbk.)
1. Akademiia russkogo baleta im. A.IA. Vaganovoi—History. 2. Ballet companies—
Russia (Federation)—Saint Petersburg—History. 3. Ballet—Russia (Federation)—
Saint Petersburg—History. 4. Ballet—Social aspects. I. Title.
GV1788.6.A37P39   2011
792.8094721—dc22   2011012173

The University Press of Florida is the scholarly publishing agency for the
State University System of Florida, comprising Florida A&M University,
Florida Atlantic University, Florida Gulf Coast University, Florida International
University, Florida State University, New College of Florida, University of
Central Florida, University of Florida, University of North Florida,
University of South Florida, and University of West Florida.

University Press of Florida
2046 NE Waldo Road
Suite 2100
Gainesville, FL 32609
http://upress.ufl.edu

In loving memory of my grandparents, Lorraine Lundstrum Mellin (Penny Pepper, Princess of Swing) and Robert A. Mellin, for never wavering in their encouragement of my love of ballet and for sharing their passion for the performing arts, you are both still strongly loved and missed; in memory of my great-aunt Dorothy Lundstrum for her lifetime dedication to the art of dance; and in memory of Richard Galla, may you continue to play Chopin among the angels.

Contents

Illustrations

Author's Note

All of the translations in this book are my own, and at times I have re-tained the Russian practice of using *imiya* and *otchestvo* (first and middle names) in reference to various individuals for variety in text and as a sign of respect.

For the sake of accuracy, I have retained the Russian spelling in the first use of all names. However, to ease the burden on the American reader, in subsequent uses I have used the shortened, Westernized versions of some names where such versions exist: Preobrajenska (instead of the Russian Preobrazhenskaya); and Kshesinska (instead of Kshessinskaya). In the case of Olga Preobrajenska, her middle names, Osipovna and Io-sifovna, are used interchangeably by those who speak of her. There is a chart of name transliterations in the index for would-be scholars seek-ing more information and for those who need to refer to the appropri-ate transliteration in pursuing reference material. I've used the *Chicago Manual of Style* Romanization rules for the citations in the notes and bibliography.

The words "School" and "Academy" are used interchangeably to refer to what is currently the Vaganova Academy of Russian Ballet on Rossi Street in St. Petersburg, sometimes referred to as ARB; in Russian, the institution is referred to using various nouns—school, academy, tekni-kum, institute—depending on the era and year.

Finally, I have left intact some instances of the Russian phrase "ballet artist" when quoting from original source material. As Altynai Asylmu-ratova explained to me, the Vaganova Academy doesn't just train people to dance, it cultivates its future graduates into "artists"—well-rounded individuals skilled in music, dance history, dramatic expression, ballet, character dance, pas de deux, and other disciplines. However, when ap-propriate I have used the term "dancer" instead of "ballet artist."

Preface

After studying ballet for ten years in the United States, I first journeyed to Leningrad in 1990 to take ballet classes from Kirov teachers on an exchange program. The Soviet Union had not yet officially collapsed, and the Russia I saw then was very much still Communist in every corner. The trip opened my eyes to the high technical standards of dance in Russia and the centuries-old traditions inside the Mariinsky Theatre. I attended a graduation performance at the Mariinsky Theatre that year and watched Uliana Lopatkina dance *Pavlova and Cecchetti*, not realizing at the time what a historical moment it was. The exposure to Russian dancers on that trip, and in observing tours by the Bolshoi and Kirov to California in ensuing years, opened my eyes to a purity in academic technique that was, in my view, both incomparable and nonexistent in the United States. The uniform training, the elite artistry, the weight of tradition all combined in a visual display of classical ballet at its pinnacle. I had never seen anything like it.

I returned to Russia in 2003 for three weeks. Russia of the twenty-first century was different from the one I had seen over a decade previously, but vestiges of the Communist system remained, and still remain today. Lack of hot water for three weeks each summer, surly shopkeepers, the double-pricing system for foreigners, a dearth of common Western goods, cheap electricity and gas, and exponentially expensive real estate are just some of the elements that characterize St. Petersburg today. Unlike the West, daily survival in Russia remains a real challenge that puts the glorious world of ballet in perspective. It becomes easy to understand at least one reason that this art form of beauty and harmony has flourished for centuries: at its height, it provides an idyllic alter-reality that allows the viewer to escape the drudgery of daily living for a few hours each night.

In 2004 I bid farewell to my Western lifestyle, my comfortable apartment and steady dollar-based paycheck, and relocated to St. Petersburg, where I lived and worked for almost six years. In the course of that half-decade, I immersed myself in the world of the Mariinsky Ballet as much as possible. As a dance writer, my first goal was to cover the Mariinsky Ballet (or the Kirov, as it is still commonly called) as a correspondent for Western publications. Early forays to the Vaganova Academy led to interviews with its artistic director, Altynai Asylmuratova, and the opportunity to observe classes. I also attended both stage and studio rehearsals inside the Mariinsky Theatre, spoke with artistic directors and choreographers, interviewed dancers and later, pedagogues. In the process I formed a number of precious friendships that I value beyond words, friendships based on mutual understanding and a shared love for this special art form. But I also slowly began to see the invisible structures on which this centuries-old tradition is based, the reverence for older generations of experienced pedagogues, the history that hangs in the air, the legacy that each new generation of dancers upholds.

Today there is a hot debate brewing among followers of the Kirov-Mariinsky Ballet about the quality of its performers. Those who witnessed the company decades ago lament the passing of some of ballet's greatest names, and with them, an entire era in Russian ballet. The repetition of this refrain from ballet-goers and critics alike caused me to consider the source of the contention. Is this great tradition actually disappearing with each subsequent decade? Or have the aesthetics and limitations of ballet itself simply shifted? More important, what do those who actually work in the Mariinsky Theatre and the Vaganova Academy think of these claims? Do they share the same observations, and if so, to what extent?

The pages that follow are my attempt to uncover at least part of the internal world of the Petersburg Ballet, and also to chronicle the thoughts and experiences of historical personages that would otherwise remain unrecorded, particularly in English. I've tried to provide adequate historical background in the first half of the book in order to place the book's second half in a more meaningful context. The information in the first two chapters was compiled from Russian source materials housed inside the Saint Petersburg Theatrical Library, adjacent to the Vaganova Academy itself. To date, little of this information exists in English. The library is perhaps the only institution in the world with a plethora of information about Vaganova's training and her life, and I made efforts to include as many details as possible without straying too far from the subject matter. While by no means comprehensive, this book aims to provide essential background information regarding the path that Agrippina Vaganova followed, from her earliest days in the halls of the Imperial Ballet School of Tsarist Russia to her years as director of the Academy in Leningrad. I hope that through these pages, Western readers will discover a closer connection to and understanding of the great woman who changed the face of Russian ballet forever.

Pedagogues' voices, in general, are rarely heard beyond theater walls. In the case of those interviewed for this book, few have ever been translated and published outside of their native language. I hope that documenting their thoughts and opinions might further enrich the readers' sense of what the Vaganova and Mariinsky traditions mean. Many of these individuals worked directly with Agrippina Yakovlevna, either as her students or as pedagogues she trained specifically to ensure the perpetuity of her training system.

Finally, I have included a short interview with Uliana Lopatkina near the end of the book. As a leading ballerina with the Mariinsky Theatre, Lopatkina remains the best definition of the Petersburg style of ballet in present-day Russia, and as such her opinions are of considerable importance to this discussion.

It is often difficult for Westerners to grasp the depth of a legacy that spans centuries. In the case of the United States, at least, the country itself is barely as old; we have no comparable great ancient traditions, especially in the realm of art. Walking the halls of the Mariinsky Theatre, inhaling the musty smell backstage, gazing at the dim lights of the silent, empty auditorium immediately lends a sense of the sacred to this building that has fostered some of ballet's greatest names. The weight of tradition hangs heavy in the air in St. Petersburg, whether inside the Vaganova Academy studios or the gilded Mariinsky Theatre. The individuals interviewed for this book grew up surrounded by these traditions on a daily basis, and that has indelibly influenced their lives, their outlook, and their opinions, if not their very souls, in a way that is difficult for outsiders to comprehend.

The information in this book sheds greater light on the phenomenon that is Vaganova training, its place in history, and its current place not only in Petersburg ballet but on the world stage as a whole. It is my deepest wish that readers will gain as much enjoyment from these pages as I did while working on this manuscript.

Acknowledgments

Although my love for Russian ballet began decades ago, without the superb language-teaching skills of Professors Andrews and Grenier at Georgetown University, this book would never have been possible. I am eternally grateful for my "Russian family," which includes Anastasia Vasilievna, for her constant support and openness, for smiles when others were frowning, and help in obtaining the final interviews for this manuscript; Grisha P., for being a forever constant, supportive friend, a creature at once more Russian and less definable than anyone I've ever met; Islom and Katya for their openness, friendship, and for providing a small oasis of comfortable, open "Western" interaction amid the sea of Russians; Sveta Ivanova for helping me to feel at home in the larger, more enriching world of the Mariinsky Theatre and for her unquestionable trust and our valuable friendship; Jill S., for becoming my best friend and partner in crime, for sharing stories of her many years in Petersburg and supporting me through the inevitable frustrations that only Westerners can understand, and for sharing in the moments of joy and small achievements in the course of working on this manuscript; Ira Fedortsova, my guardian angel many times over for her help, friendship, and understanding, for revealing to me that there is such a thing as a Western-oriented Russian in Petersburg; Anastasia Fedotova, for providing the literal key to a sacred, historical space at 93 Canal Griboedova that proved a retreat where I could write and think; Oksana Tokranova, for her endless professional support, her faith in me, her kindness and friendship; and Elena Lollo, for enduring my numerous requests and responding with prompt efficiency and professionalism to each one.

The photographs in this book are courtesy of the archives of the Mariinsky Theatre, individual photographers, and Stanislav Belyaevsky.

My gratitude to everyone for their help in providing visual support to accompany the text.

My deep appreciation to Meredith Babb for believing in this manuscript from the very start, and to everyone else at the University of Florida Press for their assistance and professionalism in helping this manuscript become a book. To Marthe Walters for her prompt efficiency, flexibility, and kind explanations throughout the final stages of the publication process; to Patterson Lamb for her patience, flexibility, and responsiveness during the copyediting process. Without all of you, this small dream would never have become a reality.

In the United States, special gratitude goes to Mary Ellen Hunt, for her friendship across oceans, enthusiastic support, keen editorial eye, selfless understanding, and for sharing both my passion for Russian ballet and, vicariously, a very special journey with me. To my big brother and close friend Nikolai Kabaniaev, who was perhaps the sole individual who supported my crazy dream of moving to Russia before I ever left the States, for his early collaboration and help with contacts as I first began this journey, and for encouraging me to write a book. To my sister Margaret, for patiently and attentively reviewing early sections of the manuscript, for her wise counsel, ongoing interest, and support in this project. To Milena Dostanich, for helping me to understand parts of the Eastern mindset, for being a true friend, and for always encouraging me to dream big. To Toba Singer, who inspired the idea for the final structure of this book; to Heather Barrett, who shared wise, practical advice and helped me navigate the publishing process. To Claudia Bauer, my long lost ballet sister, for her valuable input and help at the final stages of the manuscript. Last but most certainly not least, to my parents, for providing me space to finish this book. To all of you and countless others, I am eternally grateful.

To all of the dancers at the Mariinsky Theatre, both past and present, for upholding the traditions of Vaganova's training and style—no matter what the consensus is regarding its status—hour after hour, year after year, in the studios and onstage, for dedicating yourselves to an arguably dying art form, and for providing a world of beauty and idealism, a much preferred alternative to the harsh realities of the other world in which we live and breathe, this is for you.

Chronological History of the Vaganova Academy of Russian Ballet

1737 (Sept.)   Jean Baptiste Lande submits a request to found a dancing school in St. Petersburg.

1738 (May 4)   Anna Ivanova signs a decree opening the "Dancing School of Her Highness" (Imperial Dancing School).

1779   Reorganization/transformation of the dancing school into the Imperial Theatre School (училище = school, academy), uniting within its walls the preparation of dancers, musicians, and dramatic actors.

1809   On Didelot's initiative, a "State" of the Imperial Theatre School is taken, which officially decrees the existing ballet school and defines the goals and tasks of the academic institution, "the replacement of foreign artists with theatre pupils is one [main] focus of the establishment of this school."

1829 (10 May)   A new "State of the School" is signed, by which the goal of the Imperial Theatre School consists of "the preparation of capable and educated actors for Russian dramatic troupes, those who are skillful and know the music of singers, and singers of opera, excellent dancers and ballet dancers, and . . . orchestral musicians."

1836   The Imperial Theatre School moves from 93 Canal Griboedova to a new building on Theatre Street (Rossi Street), where Italian architect Carlo Rossi, with the help of Alberto Cavos and engineers, specially builds the first Russian ballet studio with wooden floors.

| 1847 | Marius Petipa arrives in St. Petersburg; from 1869 is balletmaster in the Mariinsky Theatre. |

1865   A new Charter, by which the Imperial Theatre School is named the Choreographic School.

1881   Prince Ivan Vsevolozhsky becomes director of the theaters. The School receives a large amount of funding in its two main divisions: ballet and dramaturgy.

1888   A new Charter by which the Imperial Theatre School defines the length of teaching children to be seven years, providing special classes in ballet, ballroom, character, divertissements, and mime. In the span of 150 years (1738–1888), already 891 students have graduated from the School, of them 626 female artists and 265 males.

1892   The School program introduces the subject, "Theory of Recording Dance," which is taught by the dancer Vladimir Ivanovich Stepanov. Enrico Cecchetti teaches at the School until 1902, reviving interest in male dancing and exposing Russia to Italian virtuosity in dance.

1896   Stepanov develops a program to teach ballet based on the students' year of study. Previously there had been no system, with lessons based on the talents of the students in a particular class or year.

1904   Mikhail Fokine begins teaching in the School; in 1907 he choreographs his first version of *Chopiniana*. In 1911 he becomes ballet master of the Mariinsky, where he remains until 1918.

1906   Girls and boys are combined in the classes of general school subjects.

1909   On Nicolas Legat's initiative, a class focusing on lifts is introduced.

1917–18   Following an interim directorship in 1917–18, Leonid

Leontiev directs the School beginning in 1918. Beginning in 1920, Alexander Alexandrovich Oblakov, a dancer of the former Mariinsky Theatre (now renamed the State Academic Theatre of Opera and Ballet), becomes artistic director of the School. On Oblakov's initiative, Olga Preobrazhenskaya is asked to set concert numbers on the stage of the School theater.

1918   The Imperial Theatre School is renamed the State Petrograd Theatrical (Ballet) School.

1920–51   Agrippina Vaganova teaches at the School.

1923   Evening classes led by Victor Alexandrovich Semenov are opened at the School. Konstantin Sergeyev, Vakhtang Chabukhiani, Feya Balabina, Zinaida Vasilieva, Sergei Korin, and Robert Gerbek, among others, enroll in the program.

1924   The School becomes the Leningrad Choreographic School.

1928   The Choreographic School publishes its first *Collection of Academic Author Programs.*

1929   Special and general educational programs are equalized. Conversion of the Choreographic School to Choreographic Teknikum (until 1937).

1930–40   Boris Vasilievich Shavrov becomes artistic director of the School.

1931   A new class in "double work," or partnering, is offered by Boris Shavrov.

1932   Famous pedagogue Alexander Pushkin begins to teach in the School.

1934   On Vaganova's initiative, a pedagogical department is opened; Agrippina Yakovlevna Vaganova publishes her book, *Osnovye Klassicheskogo Tansa* (published in English as *Basic Principles of Classical Ballet*). Also, a national division is opened that prepares special cadres from the (Soviet) Union republics for ballet theaters. Vaganova receives the prestigious title People's Artist of the USSR.

1935   The theater is renamed "Kirov" after the recently assassinated Sergei Kirov, the mayor of Leningrad.

1936–40   Fyodor Vasilievich Lopukhov is artistic director of the School.

1937   The balletmaster division is opened in the School, led by Leonid Lavrovsky. From 1937 Fyodor Lopukhov is director of this division.

1938   The 200-year anniversary of the School. Konstantin Sergeyev becomes its director. *Materials on the History of Russian Ballet* is published by M. V. Borisoglebsky under the Leningrad State Choreographic Institute.

1939   *Character Dance*, by Andrei Lopoukov, Alexander Shirayev, and Alexander Bocharov, is published.

1940–52   Nikolai Pavlovich Ivanovsky becomes artistic director of the School.

1940   The School receives the Ordain of the Red Banner of Labor. Nikolai Ivanovsky publishes *Ballroom Dance of the 16th–19th Centuries*.

1941   Evacuation to Perm.

1943 (Jan.) The first selection of students during the blockade at the Leningrad Choreographic School.

1943 (Sept.) The second selection of students during the blockade at the Leningrad Choreographic School.

1944   Return from Perm to Leningrad.

1946   Vaganova receives the Stalin Prize and is named the first professor of choreography.

1949   Graduation of Romanian and Hungarian groups; the beginning of work with the foreign division.

1951	Students perform Vasily Ivanovich Vainonen's *The Nutcracker* onstage at the Kirov Theatre for the first time.
1952–54	Tatiana Mikhailovna Vecheslova is artistic director of the School.
1954–56	Nikolai Ivanovsky is again artistic director of the School.
1957	On the initiative of Marietta Frangopulo, the School museum is opened. The School is renamed after Agrippina Vaganova.
1961	The Choreographic School receives the title "Academic."
1962–73	Feya Balabina is artistic director of the School.
1969	The book, *Lifts in The Duet,* by Nikolai Nikolaevich Serebrennikov, is published.
1973–92	Konstantin Sergeyev is artistic director of the School.
1988	The 250-year anniversary of the School. A new building and a renewed museum exhibition are opened. The first All-Russian Vaganova Competition takes place. The School receives the Ordain of Lenin.
1990	The School tours the United States for the first time.
1990	The Second All-Russian Vaganova Competition takes place.
1992	The Leningrad Choreographic School becomes the Vaganova Academy of Russian Ballet, a higher professional academic institution. Igor Belsky becomes artistic director.
1993	The Pedagogical Faculty organizes an advanced degree program for training balletmasters.
1995	The president of the Russian Federation grants the Academy the status of "especially valued object of the cultural heritage of the Russian Federation."
1996	The International Center for the Preservation and Development of Agrippina Vaganova's Method and Heritage is created, offering annual seminars.

Representatives from all Russian ballet schools and from nearby countries participate. Courses for increasing qualifications are begun. The Vaganova Prix Competition is created, and the Academy of Russian Ballet (Vaganova Academy)'s *Vestnik ARB* periodical begins its publication cycle. Choreographic training is offered by Boris Eifman and Igor Belsky at the Academy.

1998   Modern dance classes are introduced to the Academy during years five, six, and seven of training.

2007   The Academy extends its course of study from eight to nine years in length again, in order to unify the system with other European training systems.

Chronology of
Agrippina Vaganova's Life

1879 On June 27 (Old Style)

Vaganova is born into a poor family, christened Agraffina, and called Grusha by her friends. Her father, a noncommissioned officer and later an usher in the Mariinsky Theatre, dies shortly after she enrolls in the Imperial Ballet school.

1889

At age ten, Vaganova begins to attend the Imperial Ballet School.

1897 (Spring)

Graduates from the Imperial ballet school and dances two roles: Oread, the nymph in *The Trials of Damis,* or *The Pranks of Love,* and the Black Pearl in *The Pearl.* Officially Vaganova graduated in 1896 but was forced to wait one year to join the Mariinsky because of the age requirement for beginning work in the theater.

1910

Dances the Waltz in Fokine's *Chopiniana.*

1915

Dances *Giselle* for the first time.

1916

Retires from the stage. At her farewell concert dances *La Source* in the best traditions of the past, "lifting the art of Russian choreography to great heights."

1917

Begins her pedagogical practice. Works at Akim Volinsky's School of Russian Ballet, which is initially called "Baltflot."

1921

Begins work as a pedagogue at the Leningrad Choreographic Academy (formerly the Imperial Ballet School and later called the Vaganova Academy).

1922

Begins to teach the class of perfection at the State Academic Theatre of Opera and Ballet (GATOB).

1931–37

Works as Artistic Director of the Kirov Ballet. Under her reign, the following ballets choreographed by Ratislav Zakharov (to music by Boris Asafiev) enter the repertoire: *The Flames of Paris* (1932), *The Fountain of Bachchisarai* (1934), *Lost Illusions* (1936), and *Partisans Days* (1937).

1933

Restages *Swan Lake*, attempting to preserve the value of the 1894–95 production and changing some of the dramatic expression by cutting scenes that she considered heavy in pantomime. Vaganova adds several variations and alters the *port de bras* to create "swan arms," as they are known today. On Vaganova's initiative, a pedagogical department is opened; Vaganova publishes her book, *Osnovye Klassicheskogo Tantsa* (published in English as *Basic Principles of Classical Ballet.*) Also, a national division opens to prepare special cadres from the Soviet Union republics for ballet theaters.

1935

Following the trend of socialist realism, Vaganova rechoreographs *Esmeralda*, which has "more realistic stage images" than the previous version. The theater is renamed "Kirov" after the recently assassinated Sergei Kirov, the mayor of Leningrad.

1936

Receives the title of People's Artist of the Russian Soviet Federative Socialist Republic (RSFSR).

1943

Becomes a consultant for the Bolshoi Theatre in Moscow. On June 19 is awarded the title professor of choreography.

1946

Receives the Stalin Prize of the First Class, for talented achievement in the area of the art of ballet. (Later, Ulanova, Dudinskaya, Semënova, Vecheslova, Balabina, and Shelest also receive the Stalin prize.)

1951

Agrippina Vaganova dies.

Introduction

For admirers of the famously refined Mariinsky Ballet—home to many
of the world's most famous dancers and the repository of what many
consider to be the pinnacle of Russian achievement in dance—it may
come not as just a surprise but a genuine shock to hear one of the great
teachers of our time:

> Unfortunately I must declare that very little has remained of Va-
> ganova's method. The patience of pedagogues to teach children
> and adults, and the attention of the dancers to learn the coordina-
> tion, I think it is all a bit broken, and now our famous Leningrad
> Ballet School is being combined with other schools that suddenly
> come from the periphery. The actual initial students of Vaganova,
> they are, you can say, better than today's children because . . . be-
> cause they relate to it with responsibility. But for this generation of
> dancers today, for some reason it seems to me that they somehow
> decided it's not required of them, it's not necessary. And I am very
> upset about this.

One might expect a product of the Soviet system like Ninella Kurgapkina—the famous spitfire ballerina—to perhaps blindly support the
system she herself has helped to preserve, but Kurgapkina's opinions are
surprisingly candid. With a diploma in choreography and considerable
teaching credits, she remains one of the preeminent names in Russian
ballet circles, a ballerina who danced with Rudolf Nureyev before his
defection, and one graced with the titles Honored Artist of the RSFSR

(1957), People's Artist of the RSFSR (1966), and People's Artist of the USSR (1974).

A small woman with straight, often uncombed gray hair, void of makeup and jewelry, and more reminiscent of a country peasant than a decorated former ballerina, Kurgapkina is unhesitating in her frankness. She spoke at length about Agrippina Vaganova's role in the traditions of the Mariinsky Theatre and Academy of Russian Ballet—now known as the Vaganova Academy—at our meeting just two weeks before her death in May 2009. Her staunch, unyielding opinions about the great pedagogue are quite unguarded, but as I discovered, she is not alone in her criticisms of the recent evolution of the great Vaganova school and the pedagogues who guard Vaganova's legacy.

Still, others take a longer view. Tatiana Terekhova—a famous ballerina and pedagogue in her own right—declares that while some elements may have been lost over time, the core values of Vaganova training still continue to produce superior dancers with honed artistry and crisp technique.

Who was this woman, Agrippina Vaganova, and how did she manage to leave such an indelible imprint on Russian classical ballet? How has her name influenced so many people and been linked with such a deep cultural tradition? And why is the continuation of the traditions she instilled such a hotbed of debate, even today?

~

Born in 1879, when the tsars still ruled in Russia, Agrippina Yakovlevna Vaganova was a modern woman for her generation. Unlike other dancers from her era, Vaganova's country, culture, and the time when she came into her art all conspired to create a legendary figure who would leave an indelible mark on Russian ballet and become a name known worldwide. Her long life spanned several periods in Russia, and the legacy she left behind as the codifier of the Vaganova method of ballet training is now recognized internationally for its contributions to the art of ballet. With her death in 1951, well after her country had adopted and instilled the Communist Party as its dominant political system, an epoch in Russian ballet ended. Since then, many of Vaganova's own pupils have completed successful stage careers and are now coaching today's leading ballerinas. Several individuals who were trained directly by Agrippina Yakovlevna herself to become pedagogues are now in their eighties, still teaching at the Vaganova Academy of Russian Ballet in Saint Petersburg.

Some of the best names in ballet have trained under Vaganova's methodology: Rudolf Nureyev, Mikhail Baryshnikov, Yuri Soloviev, Irina Kolpakova, and Natalia Makarova among them. Each dancer studied at the famed Academy on Rossi Street in Petersburg—or Petrograd, or Leningrad, depending on its name in a given year—and each went on to become a legend of sorts in his or her own right.

"Vaganova training" carries with it great prestige. Graduates of the Academy are offered employment contracts with the best international ballet companies. Not infrequently, a member of the Mariinsky corps de ballet will be given a soloist or principal contract elsewhere in the world, pointing to the high standards of training, the clean technique that dancers acquire from the Academy. And yet, when we refer to "Vaganova training" today, it is with the understanding that we credit those many important pedagogues who continued the work of Vaganova after her death, for they are not only part of her legacy but are now the proverbial carriers of her torch for future generations of ballet artists.

Before Vaganova, what system of training existed in Russia? In the 1800s, teachers from Italy and France brought their own traditions and teachings to the Russian stage. With them, both French and Italian ballerinas performed in Russia, gaining enormous popularity in Petersburg. Names such as Pierina Legnani, Virginia Zucchi, and Carlotta Brianza were well known to the theatergoing public of the 1880s and 1890s, but they were not Russian dancers. The French school at the end of the nineteenth century was characterized by overly decorative movements described by Vaganova as "saccharine sweetness" with flaccid poses and limited virtuosity.[1] The Italian school, on the other hand, according to Vaganova, focused on virtuosity at the expense of poetry and substance.[2] The main guides to classical ballet included the four-volume issue of *The Letters about Dance* by Noverre, published upon the order of Tsar Alexander I in 1803–1804, and Carlo Blasis's *The Code of Terpsichore*, published in 1828, which codified existing French technique and laid the foundation for the Italian school. Russia had nothing systematized or codified of its own.

The result was a mix of styles, but an uncategorized and unstandardized one. The idea of focusing on the process of teaching ballet was unique at the turn of the nineteenth century and had not been done in Russia before. Vaganova's efforts to take the best from the existing knowledge, improve upon it, systemize it, and further develop virtuosic technique was unprecedented in Russia. She worked to teach dancers a conscious approach to each movement. Her students not only learned steps, but the reason for them and how they should be executed. Vaganova's work gradually set in place an ideal standard for what became known as the distinctly "Russian" school. Through trial and error, and research, Vaganova prompted her pupils to find the reasons behind unsuccessful execution of steps, thereby instilling a standard execution and a new, more conscious approach to ballet movements that would become the backbone of the strongest ballet tradition in the world.

In the end, the Vaganova system taught dancers to dance with the entire body to acquire harmony of movement and to expand their range of expression.[3] This ideal harmony, characterized by a pliant, flexible back, well-articulated *port de bras*, emotionally vibrant expression, and strong, clean footwork is now recognized the world over as a sign of Vaganova training.

I

Vaganova the Dancer

From the writings of those who saw her as a child, as a dancer on stage, and later as a teacher—individuals such as famed dance historian Ludmila Blok or dance critic Akim Volinsky—and from those who worked with Vaganova during her lifetime, we can begin to learn something about Agrippina Yakovlevna Vaganova's life path. Her start in ballet has much in common with the beginnings of other dancers: years of daily training at the ballet barre, classes, rehearsals, and finally performances. Vaganova entered the Imperial Ballet School of Russia in 1889, before the Russian Revolution that would permanently alter the structure of her society; she danced on stage before World War I tore her country in half. And she began to teach at a time when Soviet ideology had taken firm root in Russia, affecting not only politics but art as well.

One of three daughters born to a father who was a noncommissioned officer, and later an usher and box-keeper at the Mariinsky Theatre, Vaganova had early exposure to the theater. The Vaganova family was poor, and a child's acceptance to the Imperial Ballet School meant one less mouth to feed. She was christened Agraffina, called Grusha by her girlfriends, but used the name Agrippina throughout her life.

"The career of Agrippina Yakovlevna Vaganova, as that of any dancer's, began at age ten when she joined the school," writes Ludmila Blok, renowned Russian ballet historian and critic. "This is truly already the beginning of a career: one has to be better than others, one has to win. For some, it is external traits [that help them]; for others, powerful protection. Vaganova didn't have any sort of protection, even the very weakest sort. She won over the examiners Ekaterina Ottovna Vazem and Pavel Alexandrovich Gerdt with the . . . agile legs of a ten-year-old child."[1] When Blok speaks of protection, she refers to influence and clout. Unlike her near-contemporary Matilda Kshessinskaya, mistress of the Tsarevich, Vaganova had none of the so-called outside connections that could help her career. Her path, from the very beginning, was one of plain, old-fashioned hard work.

While still a student at the Imperial Ballet School, Vaganova spent summers at the government dacha at Tsarskoe Selo, also known as Catherine the Great's Summer Palace, near the city of Pushkin on the outskirts of Petersburg. Groups of students from the school would travel there for the summer holidays, where morning ballet classes were given. Blok claims that, unlike her classmates, Agrippina Yakovlevna rehearsed herself all summer long, so that the autumnal return to the ballet studio was not a shock to her legs as it was for the other girls. It seems that Agrippina's stern work ethic was evident early on.

The training structures at the former Imperial Ballet School, called the Leningrad Choreographic Institute during the Soviet years, comprised a dual system that incorporated the two dominant styles of dance at the time, French and Italian. The Russian dancers were known for their rich emotionality, but a specific Russian style of ballet had not yet been established. However, the Russian ballet of the 1890s, the atmosphere that surrounded Vaganova at the time, was characterized by the creation of some of ballet's greatest works, with scores by Tchaikovsky and Glazunov and choreography by Marius Petipa and Lev Ivanov, who would become known worldwide for their choreography in ensuing years.

In seven years at the School, the young Vaganova studied sequentially with Alexander Oblakov, Lev Ivanov, Ekaterina Vazem, Christian Johansson, and Pavel Gerdt.[2] Then, as now, the final year of study was considered the most important in the dancers' training, as it prepared and positioned them for life in the theater. Even today, Vaganova graduates are identified by the pedagogue under whom they graduated— "one of Safronova's students" or "he graduated under Seliutskiï"—even

though that teacher may have coached them only during their las
years, or even just the final ten months of their time in the School.

As critic Yuri Slonimsky noted, the 1890s were also the beginning
historical shift in Russian ballet when an "uneasy generation born thi.
ing for the new" appeared.[3] Some considered the new generation a thre.
to Russia's heritage of traditional classical ballet, while others found it a
necessary, modernizing source of revitalization. But those events were
still to come.

Vaganova's first teacher was Alexander Oblakov, a tall, slender, well-
dressed man whose utterly erect posture inspired rumors that he wore a
corset. Vaganova notes in her memoirs how soft-spoken Oblakov was—
and how little she learned from him. From there she graduated to the
class of Lev Ivanov, noting that his lesson was lazily led, the program ill-
defined, and the results, if any, meager at best. She subsequently worked
with Ekaterina Vazem at length.

It is in reference to Vazem that we first hear of Vaganova's great enthusiasm for a teacher. "Unusually strict and demanding," Vaganova wrote,
"she immediately stunned the participants who were used to apathy and
the complete indifference of Ivanov's class."[4]

Vaganova wrote about how Vazem directed her lessons:

> Vazem approached dance training in the sternest manner. She ap-
> proached the development of strength in the legs by means of tech-
> nically developed squats and *plié*, working the torso and partially
> the arms to develop softness. No matter how big the class was, she
> always saw everyone; no one slipped from her view. Here we en-
> countered serious teaching, and the incapable students, who were
> not dismissed after the first year [as was usually done] ended up
> in a difficult situation, as grasping all of the subtleties of choreo-
> graphic art [using] their natural traits wasn't possible. . . . My fate
> emerged in Vazem's class completely unexpectedly for me.[5]

Vazem's demanding nature forced even the lazy students to shape up, but
for Vaganova, who thrived doing systematic work, Vazem's classes were
a sincere joy. Vaganova would later emulate several of Vazem's qualities:
by nature Agrippina Yakovlevna, too, was strict and demanding, and she
did not overlook a single student in her own classroom. Vazem demonstrated that it was impossible to construct classes simply by imitating

a teacher's movement, without an analysis of each movement into its component parts.[6] This early conscious, analytical, and nearly technical approach to dancing, one that required thought and the student's self-application to the lesson, no doubt influenced Vaganova's later training methods.

Instead of spending the requisite three years with Vazem, Vaganova received nine points out of twelve on her exam that year and was moved ahead, skipping a year of study.

From there Vaganova joined the class of Christian Johansson, a seventy-year-old Swedish-born teacher, beloved by his students. Vaganova gained additional technical knowledge from him but was frustrated at the lack of analysis and explanation during lessons:

> What did Johansson's class give me? I began to do more jumps, so-called *batterie*. . . . We learned several movements in a circle, but how to do them wasn't explained. A year of such training led to some sort of results. Receiving 10 points at the exam, I entered the older class by the same pedagogue. . . . As much as possible, near the approach of the end of our dancing education, they gave us more difficult movements, more jumps and pointework, but alas, this took place without explanation.[7]

Even before graduation, Vaganova thirsted for greater understanding of the reasons for movements, their initiation and execution, a trait that would appear later in her teaching career.

Vaganova received an eleven out of twelve on her exam that year, thus completing the course of study at age sixteen. This posed a problem because dancers had to be at least seventeen and a half years old to be accepted into the Mariinsky Ballet at that time. As a result, Vaganova spent the interim year continuing to study ballet at the School, but free from the requirements of academic courses, which she had already completed. She wrote:

> At this time an event took place at the ballet school. They decided to undertake reforms of the ballet classes (which for some reason only concerned the women's classes). An Italian artist invited by the directorship appeared named Enrico Cecchetti. During this period the directorship was resorting to various means to develop

the art of ballet, inviting Italian ballerinas and Moscow ballerinas to guest. Although the ballet in Moscow was not radiant, there were two ballerinas, (Ekaterina Vasilievna) Geltser and (Lubov Andreyevna) Roslavleva. On the Mariinsky stage . . . there were no brilliant dancers.

The performance of Cechetti introduced a big revival. He was not a young dancer, but he amazed the artists and the viewers with the virtuous movements of the Italian school.

Instead of arms with sagging elbows (the so-called French manner of the time), Cecchetti's style was quite different. The poses became more dynamic, more assured, and the Italian aplomb appeared; true, at times it revealed inadequately refined, bent legs in jumps (the typical manner of Italian jumps of the period). But at that time, when even other inadequacies of the Italian school were completely outdated, it seemed interesting and new.

An insistent person, Cecchetti was insistent in his teaching too. . . . Each ballet artist dreaming of a career drifted to his class, but it cost quite a bit at that time (thirty rubles per month), and far from everyone could allow themselves that.

. . . With one year left of school, I received my first visible place in the so-called student graduation performance. I danced a divertissement, the solo part in the gallop of *La Fille Mal Gardée*. . . . Cecchetti saw me. Evidently he found something interesting in me, for he expressed a desire to include me in the list of his students, but he was refused: I had only one year to graduation, and he was given students for a two-year [trial] period, to prove [the worth of] his pedagogical methods. I broke into tears. It seemed to me that all was lost, and truly it prevented me from more successfully beginning my stage career.[8]

For that final year, 1896, Vaganova was taught by Pavel Andreevich Gerdt, a representative of the French manner of dancing that Vaganova disliked. Her writings offer her observations of Cecchetti's methods, classes, and students. Unable to take Cecchetti's classes, the most Vaganova could do was observe them in her free moments and try to recall what she saw. Even then, Vaganova wanted to study and perfect herself, but opportunities for this were few.[9]

Blok noted that "the differences between the two styles were striking: on the one hand, the calm, traditional lessons of the French school, on the other hand the temperamental, bold lessons of the Italians."[10] Indeed, the Italian ballerinas of the time were known for their virtuosity, cultivating "aplomb, dynamic turns, and the strength and endurance of the toes,"[11] but they were seen by many as lacking in poetry and content. Nonetheless, the Italian school gained renown while Cecchetti worked in Petersburg, with leading ballerinas such as Anna Pavlova traveling to Milan for his lessons.

Vaganova aspired to penetrate the secrets of the Italian school on her own. Her natural traits—strong, smooth, certain legs—helped her. But history records that her arms were by nature "dry and inflexible—they resisted [being properly trained]. Overcoming them was harder."[12] And in terms of her looks, Vaganova's appearance bothered her: she had large, hard features, and "onstage this powerful face lost expressive movement. . . . She was also large in relation to the short-statured dancers of the time. Muscular legs, wide shoulders, a straight spine . . . the vulgar lines of her arms as if already refuting grace."[13] Despite these physical inadequacies, Vaganova was determined to develop herself into a better dancer. But to do so she had to unlock the secrets of successful dancing at the time. As Cecchetti's students began to achieve great success, Vaganova strove to master this new, Italian technique. Blok writes:

> Agrippina Yakovlevna remembers with a smile what difficulty a double tour seemed to all of the other students and to her, when they tried even from afar to see this step through the door cracks, beginning with a sharp plié, [a step] so unfamiliar and worthy of envy.
>
> Her love for work and ability to boil down a movement to its very essence were inborn traits that perfectly matched her career as pedagogue extraordinaire.[14]

The bravura manner of the Italian school only served to whet Vaganova's appetite. She wanted not only to learn the steps themselves but also how to approach them. In this area, another one of Agrippina Yakovlevna's early teachers influenced her greatly. Olga Iosifovna (Osipovna) Preobrazhenskaya (or Preobrajenska as she is known in the West) helped cultivate Vaganova's curiosity regarding the best approach to steps and form. During her study with Preobrajenska, Vaganova began to think about how to judiciously clarify the movement, force the entire body to work, subdue all of the muscles into working.[15] These early attempts at analysis were also attempts to unify the French and the Italian methods into another distinct form.

Preobrajenska's influence on Vaganova's teaching is perhaps less well-known in the West, but it is important to acknowledge. This ballerina who studied under Marius Petipa, Lev Ivanov, and Christian Johansson, graduated in 1889 from the Imperial Ballet School, although she was dismissed and readmitted twice during her course of study for health reasons.

While still dancing at the Mariinsky, Preobrajenska began to teach in 1914. From 1917 to 1920 she taught "plastika" to the opera artists at the Mariinsky and led classical lessons at the "Baltflot" school (or "Baltic Navy School" as it was initially called; it was listed under the patronage of Baltic sailors). The school was better known later as Akim Volinsky's School of Russian Ballet, where Vaganova herself would initially teach as well. Unfortunately, however, the school accepted students without audition, for Volinsky thought that anyone desiring to become a ballet artist should not be turned away.[16] Preobrajenska left the stage in 1920. In 1921 she emigrated, teaching in Milan, London, Buenos Aires, and Berlin. Beginning in 1923 she taught at her own studio in Paris. It should be noted that Paris and its environs had scores of ballet schools at the time, but Preobrajenska's school achieved such a reputation that the most famous ballerinas considered it an honor to study with her.[17] It was here that she trained two of the three "baby ballerinas" chosen by George Balanchine as stars of the first post-Diaghilev Ballets Russes company: Tamara Toumanova and Irina Baranova. In their own way, these two women absorbed some of the Imperial ballet traditions and brought them further west.

Preobrajenska's dancing was characterized by a "sincerity of execution"[18] according to Nina Tikanova, one of her students: "She danced in a miraculous way, incorporating both plastique and gracefulness. Not blessed by nature with a jump, she was still endlessly light, while in movement and soul she achieved a thrilling veracity."[19]

Preobrajenska dedicated herself to the pedagogical profession in Paris, strictly preserving the traditions and covenant of the Russian school as it existed at the time. Her talent, endless love for her art, and unlimited kindness were notable.[20] Mikhail Fokine set the Prelude in his famous ballet *Les Sylphides* specifically for Preobrajenska. Nijinska too was "fascinated" by the "dainty pizzicato pas" that Preobrajenska danced in *La Source*.[21]

Vaganova studied with Preobrajenska in Petersburg at the Imperial Ballet School. Firsthand accounts of the ballerina's teaching methods shed light on traits that may have reappeared in Vaganova's method.

Vera Kostrovitskaya wrote about Preobrajenska's classes in her 1978 book, *Mastera Baleta Samodeiatelnosti—Metodicheskiye Posobie* (Masters of Amateur Ballet—A Learning Guidebook):

> To the time of my attendance in the Petrograd Ballet school [1916], famous pre-revolutionary teachers such as P[avel] Gerdt and N[icolas] Legat no longer existed. Of the ballerinas, only Olga Osipovna Preobrajenska taught . . .
>
> I can judge Preobrajenska's lessons only by my childhood memories, as I studied under her during my first year and a few months of my second year in the school. I recall, for example, that we stood facing the barre for just a few days, after which we worked with one hand on the barre. From the very beginning, Preobrajenska demanded full turnout of the leg in each classical position. In *battements tendus*, upon closing the "working" leg into fifth position, she taught us to lightly bend the knee so that the accent into fifth on the floor was achieved. The acceptance of this completely contradicts Vaganova, who said the leg must move in opposition with an absolutely straightened knee.
>
> . . . During lessons, Preobrajenska didn't sit on a chair, but showed us the steps herself. . . . I do not recall a single pedagogue aside from Elizabeth Gerdt who was so particularly charming and so beautifully showed the steps in lessons as Preobrajenska did.[22]

Preobrajenska's class was noted to have other distinctions as well, including the simplicity of exercises *en pointe*, done first at a slow tempo and later with increasing speed, with strict attention paid to fifth position.[23] Preobrajenska's student, Yuri (later George) Zorich, noted that at her Paris school, Preobrajenska never canceled classes and spent a great deal of time attending to the smallest details, like clean footwork, turnout through first position, and arms. "She always paid attention to coordination and the synchronicity of arms, the movement of the wrists, the position of the head, including *épaulement*. Truly, after her lessons, each student could do any choreography and execute all movements with the same consistency that this or that choreographer demanded."[24] Others noted how her classes developed elasticity, muscle strength, and endurance. Her students executed movements that other pedagogues gave only at much higher levels, resulting in dancers more advanced than their counterparts. Further, Preobrajenska was said to never lift her voice or scream at her students.[25] Asaf Messerer observed Olga Preobrajenska's classes in Paris, and recorded his observations.

Peeking in on Kshesinska's class, I understood that she taught simply on a surface level. Giving a combination, she didn't even watch to see how the students executed it, but instead turned to chat with guests. Later she asked, "Well, did you finish? Ok then let's move on." It seemed that she wasn't teaching so much as spending time.

From [Kshesinska's] class, I hurried to the class of Olga Iosifovna Preobrajenska. This woman worked seriously and for the sake of earning a living. In her class, as in Kshesinska's, the public was the most mixed. "We are completely independent from the students," explained Preobrajenska, "from their freedom. Many of them combine ballet classes with work on the side. Many of them travel, going to Paris for a month or a few days."

Of course, in such a situation achieving a high level of artistic results is quite difficult. Preobrajenska hardly aimed further than that. However, her class was constructed with movement combinations that were judicious. In them you could see the Petersburg "roots."

It seemed to me that Preobrajenska's class resembled that of Vaganova's—the same orientation to study, to the knowledge of ballet principles.

Preobrajenska had to work a lot. She gave her classes in the morning, evening and daytimes. She gave corrections delicately, almost timidly, but she ran around the studio swiftly to correct students and demonstrate.[26]

Despite the quirks of her training methods—the bent knees in fifth position, for example—Preobrajenska taught Vaganova a great deal about teaching. From Preobrajenska's own comments on Isadora Duncan, we can surmise some of the ballerina's staunch views on classicism in ballet:

> "Unfortunately I haven't been able to see Duncan dance," Preobrajenska said, "but insofar as one can judge . . . from what I have seen, it seems to me there is nothing new in her art. It is the revival of the old, on which all ballet is based, and only that. The secret of her success lies in the originality of the costume and the lighting and in other purely external effects. If you subtract all of the above-mentioned points, and bring Duncan to a typical stage, clothe her in a leotard and deprive her of these accessories, the interest in the dancer will fade and boredom will threaten. There is no doubt that modern ballet is much better [now], but unfortunately its inadequacies are sensed."[27]

In her memoir, *La Jeune Fille en Bleu*, Nina Tikanova recorded the experience of taking classes with Preobrajenska, mentioning another connection between the older teacher and Vaganova. Of Preobrajenska, Tikanova wrote:

> Olga Osipovna was the personification of the epoch of Marius Petipa and considered a favorite of his. As an artist of exceptional sensitivity, she crystallized the artistry of the great master in his form and preserved it. . . .
> In Paris, dedicating herself to pedagogy, she shared her knowledge with inspiration in the theater "Olympus" where the Spanish chansons alternated with magicians and animal charmers, where the wonderful art of Petipa continued to bloom during a period when ballet suffered a visible metamorphosis.[28]
> . . . In her class exercises, especially the *port de bras*, she left the dry conventionality of the canon behind, something she insisted on decisively.[29]

However, Petipa was not the only influence on Preobrajenska's teaching. Mikhail Fokine's impressionistic methods influenced her methods as well: Preobrajenska often asked her students to improvise to music at the end of class, which taught them to think independently and developed their imagination. She also often composed dances for student concerts and for graduation performances. Her compositions were distinguished by "exceptional musicality, a sense of style that always took into consideration the individual characteristics of the student."[30] All of this left a strong impression on Vaganova the student. In her memoirs, Agrippina Yakovlevna recalled Preobrajenska's work ethic and dancing:

> What an exceptionally persistent toiler, a strict artist Olga Iosifovna Preobrajenska was! For her no difficulties existed when she achieved artistic goals. And how she transformed on stage! Any beauty without her talent would have faded. Her face inspired, barely having come onstage, barely touching the floor with her toes. The grace of movement attracted attention of the audience so much that it was impossible to take your eyes off of her.[31]

Vera Krasovskaya recorded Vaganova's own comments regarding Preobrajenska's influence on the Vaganova methodology:

> Olga Iosifovna (Preobrajenska) helped Vaganova. . . . This example of a hardworking, strict artist and one of the most businesslike tutors was left to her. "At the slightest chance," Vaganova said, "I used the wise remarks and instructions of Olga Iosifovna Preobrajenska. Her judicious explanation of the Italian exercises forced my body to work in a new way, activating every muscle that had been dormant up until then. Those few lessons that I took with her led me to a single journey, forcing me to think in dance, and to approach each movement with great consciousness."[32]

Agrippina Yakovlevna's acknowledgment of this influence gives credit to one among many of those who influenced not only her dancing style, but ultimately her own pedagogical method.

~

During her graduation performance, Vaganova danced in two ballets. She was Oread, the nymph in *The Trials of Damis* or *The Pranks of Love* (*Les Ruses d'Amour*), and the Black Pearl in *The Pearl*. She "earned great praise from such great masters of dance as Marius Petipa and Christian Johansson"[33] for the performance. Upon graduation, she joined the Mariinsky Theatre, but her road to ballerina was far from direct. In the words of Ludmila Blok, she was

forgotten for several years in the corps de ballet. A humble, poor girl, formerly without powerful protection, at 17 years of age was thrown into the wild forest of ballet intrigues, ill-will and open animosity to any new talent—she had nothing except talent in her defense. Her talent for many years persistently led her steadily up to the first row of the splendid troupe. But the path was difficult! It is true that in the density of the corps de ballet, the critics immediately recognized and began to systematically pick out Vaganova in the "Waltz" of *The Nutcracker*, where, "Vaganova stood out, [and] with her lightness and strength can boldly be listed in the ballet guard."[34]

However, it was Vaganova's appearance in *Flora's Awakening* alongside Anna Pavlova in 1900 that drew her first significant mention. On September 12, 1900, the Petersburg newspaper Teatralnoye Echo recorded that "In *Flora's Awakening*, aside from Miss Pavlova, Miss Vaganova distinguished herself, dancing boldly, and with airy lightness. Our ballet-masters have not used this dancer enough."[35]

As the Russian ballet critic and historian Galina Kremshevskaya pointed out, although the review pleased Vaganova, it carried the implication of a theme that would repeat itself throughout her career: that of the administration's indifference toward her.[36]

Finding her place within the theater and within the Mariinsky repertoire proved to be a challenge for Vaganova. At the time, Marius Petipa and his ballets still reigned, although that would change in short order. In his diary, Petipa himself referred to Vaganova only three times, twice writing that she was "horrible," and once (February 11, 1903) recording her participation as a soloist in the Shades scene of his *Bayadère*. Ballet historians Igor Slonimsky and Vadim Gaevsky agreed on why she was cast so rarely in many of the pageantry-based ballets at the time:

Now it becomes clear where and why Vaganova triumphed and suited Petipa, and where she failed and angered him. The parade-like coronation of the performance [in *The Pearl*] was not for her. . . . Also, roles in which she was either a confidante or a friend were difficult psychologically for her. From birth she was a ballerina. She was cultivated as a ballerina, that is, a dancer of high level. And the class she led in the theater was called the "ballerina's class." In this was she was Petipa's heiress, in affirmed domineering ballerina roles.[37]

Vaganova was not a Fokine ballerina either. Expression and artistry were not her natural strengths. While Nicolas Legat himself had felt the influence of the Italian school on his own French-based training, and while Vaganova, as one of his students during her theater years, also carried the "continuity of the French school,"[38] the following era, that of Fokine, brought with it a new style, an impressionistic basis for the imagery onstage. "Fokinism," as it were, pulled the male dancer forward and put him on the same level as the female; adagio become of equal value to both genders, without obliterating the helpful position of the cavalier, which eliminated the exaggerated Salon manner [aristocratic and noble] of gallantry in dance.[39] Ironically, as Vaganova would later support renovation and revolution in ballet, Fokine preferred his own dancers who were amenable to his own style, and when Diaghilev's company left to tour the West, Vaganova was not invited to accompany them. Krasovskaya remarked:

She understood that Fokine's impressionistic compositions, his pantomime saturated with dramatism were completely not her area. Meanwhile Fokine considered Vaganova the clean water of academism, and he went around her. . . . Fokine stood out not as a nihilist, but as a delicate stylizer of classical dance. At first glance it was paradoxical: an academic dancer was kin to the creative boldness of the choreographer. Meanwhile, out of devotion to tradition, Vaganova was alien and morose to the uncritical dogmatism and the limited nature, the spiritual inflexibility of some pedants. Intertwined in her character were an intolerance of impulse and unlimited patience, stubborn will and wise pliability, [and] the capability to insist that one respect another's views, if they deserved it.[40]

Agrippina Vaganova in *Chopiniana*. She was complimented for the mood she gave the dance but was said not to have been a Fokine-type dancer. Photo: Mariinsky Theatre Archives.

Despite their differences, however, the two souls managed to find common ground in Fokine's revised version of the stylized romantic ballet, *Chopiniana*, known in the West as *Les Sylphides*. *Chopiniana* was performed on March 11, 1908, at a charity performance. It was indeed impressionism on stage, the idea of a painting come to life. The main sylphide at the premiere was Anna Pavlova, who danced alongside Tamara Karsavina and Olga Preobrajenska. Vaganova learned all three roles and two years later, in 1910, danced the waltz, "after which they began to speak of her soft arms, the mood she gave the performance."[41] The last-minute replacement for an injured Karsavina, Vaganova was not first cast; she managed well in the performance, as noted above, but Kremshevskaya explains that the style was not hers:

> . . . In *Chopiniana* Anna Pavlova and Tamara Karsavina shone brightly, but not Vaganova. The ballet went down in her name, her performance was accepted, but it did not address the norms that appeared to her reviewers. Or even to her. If you saw Vaganova in a ballet, then it was in answer to all of the canonical rules, and not in the poetic miniatures of Fokine.

Nonetheless, Fokine's *Chopiniana*, judging by the reviews, gave Vaganova a great deal. After her dancing, people began to speak of her soft arms, and of the atmosphere that she had learned to give to her performance.

> Was Vaganova the ideal Sylphide? Of course not. But her musicality, the significance of the dance, broadly and boldly, impressed. *Chopiniana* was the first ballet that she danced. She was already listed along with the first soloists. The critics admired her variation. Everyone was persistently indignant at the delay in her promotion to ballerina. Everyone railed even more that they were not allowing her to dance the ballet [for those two years].[42]

Despite this early recognition, during her first years in the theater Vaganova found little inspiration from her position with the company. Her diary reflects these sentiments:

> Work in the corps de ballet did not inspire me. Looking at the virtuosity of dance acquired by Cecchetti's students, I began to sense the inadequacies of technique. In the meantime, blind imitation

did not please me. The sorrow of dissatisfaction began and [it] oppressed me.[43]

In 1901, Vladimir Arkadievich Telyakovsky's appointment as director of the Imperial Theatres altered some of the internal processes at the Mariinsky. Dancers were now allowed to appear in new roles by auditioning for them.[44] In this manner Vaganova herself was able to expand her repertoire. She danced the classical Hungarian divertissement in *Raymonda* and the quartet in *Daughters Mikado* in 1902. She later appeared in numerous ballets, including *Harlequinade* in a quartet with Anna Pavlova, Yulia Sedova, and Apollinaria Gordova; in the interpolated *pas de deux* from *La Fille Mal Gardée*; the fresco of animated statues in *The Little Humpbacked Horse*; the Queen of the Dryads in *Don Quixote*; and many others. Finally on November 10, 1910, there was that performance of *Chopiniana*, which, as Blok noted, brought "delight to many spectators and many minutes of happiness to Vaganova herself."[45]

Vaganova danced one of the Shades variations from *La Bayadère* in 1911 and received warm praise for her performance in the *Petersburg Page* (September 19): "The lightness in her *cabrioles* is rare. She flies directly, without wings or airplanes. We were told that this artist learned the entire ballet, *La Source*, long ago. But they won't let her dance it. Insulting. To see Miss Vaganova in a ballerina role would be very interesting."[46]

She managed to finally appear in that, her first big ballet, *La Source*, set by Nicolas Legat, on November 29, 1911. Blok wrote:

> For the first act Vaganova displayed an airy lightness in her amazing *balloné*; for the second act, bright footwork; for the *pas de deux* of the third act, she danced a variation of the old type, circling the entire stage with *cabrioles* in *arabesque*, and *arabesques*. The coda was brilliant, a sort of *fouetté* (*temps levé* with a turn). Of course they gave her few rehearsals and only one stage rehearsal—harsh conditions for preparation. But Vaganova's partner and teacher, Nicolas Legat, worked willingly and at length with her on this individual role. For the performance Legat sent her a bouquet with "to my best student" written on the ribbon. At that time this was audacious and a big challenge: Kshesinska was among his students. Kshesinska, mistress of her position, used all of her power to squeeze Vaganova

out as far as possible. The public knew all of the adversity towards Vaganova behind the wings, and in warm ovations she felt the share of their protest and indignation.[47]

While focusing on her career, the young Vaganova encountered the intrigues of ballet theater life just as today's dancers do. Agrippina made veiled reference to the romantic liaison between Kshesinska and the Tsarevich, and Kshesinska's subsequent dominance inside the theater in one of her own diary entries:

> Mathilde Kshesinska, whose career took shape in a most unique fashion, danced in *Paquita*. In her third year in the theater she had already danced the leading role in *The Sleeping Beauty*, and she danced whatever she wanted. . . . Life in the theater passed in a fixed manner. The young tsar with his young wife visited the theater, especially the ballet. . . .
>
> [Preobrajenska] was a contemporary of Kshesinska, but their paths were different, the first had to struggle on the road of sincere effort, and not by means of external connections.[48]

Despite the politics, Vaganova managed to carve a name for herself in history, perhaps in an unforeseen manner, but nonetheless by maintaining a steely focus on her art.

Later reviews of Agrippina's dancing became even more positive. Of her efforts in Petipa's Pas de Trois from *Paquita*, she was lauded for her "brilliant sparkle of footwork in flight, in *entrechat six*. The artist lifts off the floor like a bird. And in the air it is as if she weaves her legs in a web, crossing them unusually quickly. Her entire body is alive."[49] Of the second scene of *Swan Lake*, when she danced the *pas de deux* with Legat, critic Akim Volinsky observed:

> All of Vaganova and Legat's *pas de deux* take place under an overall feeling of surprise in the auditorium. The female artist here is at the height of her phenomenal gifts of dance, and already during her life has almost become a legend. . . . Her turnout is ideal. Her movements become entire schemes of amazing completeness. Every detail of Vaganova's is a small world of choreography, distinguished by its amazing appropriateness and consistency, so in

order to evaluate the phenomenal artist, the science of the art of dance itself must be measured, which cannot be done within the framework of one article.[50]

Likewise, of a range of divertissements performed at a gala, one Petersburg paper noted, "The best of them was a waltz created by Legat; Vaganova danced it with great lightness and even with emotion."[51] Though it may not have had the impact of Vaganova's association with Preobrajenska or Vazem, her work with Legat is nonetheless noteworthy, for his influence both as a pedagogue and as Vaganova's partner on stage.

One of two brothers, Nicolas Gustavovich Legat was identified with the old, classical, and predominantly French style of dancing. After a considerable stage career at the Mariinsky and experience partnering some of its best ballerinas, he began to choreograph and was appointed assistant balletmaster in 1902 and chief balletmaster in 1910. However, Legat's ballets were not as successful as Fokine's new works, partly because Legat relied on the old style of dance, while the theater was edging ever closer to novel ways of movement that would transform dance in Russia in the 1920s.

Despite his open conflict with Fokine and his resistance to the new, Legat nonetheless was a notable pedagogue. His teaching style was characterized by an intuitive, individual approach to each student, and by his forgiving nature. "Legat wisely thought that a person is not a machine and changes each day. He endlessly varied movements, giving new combinations,"[52] wrote Fyodor Lopukhov, who also noted:

The system of Legat conquered insofar as the venerable Johansson made him his deputy. Ballerinas came to study under Legat, and pedagogues of the school under Gerdt began to adopt his system. Vaganova became a big follower of Legat. From his class all of the "stars" began to appear: Kshesinska, Preobrajenska, Trefilova, Sedova, Karsavina, Kyaksht, Egorova, and the very young Spessivtseva. Fokine began to lead the women's class in the school, and working by Legat's system, launched new ballerinas: . . . [Elena] Lukom, and Lydia Lopukhova became famous. Fokine . . . valued [Legat] as an intelligent and talented pedagogue, of which he spoke aloud more than once. The venerable Petipa often came to Legat's classes, and encouragingly peeked his head in when Legat clarified why, at the present moment, he was giving a specific movement. Petipa, a former teacher himself, took Legat's innovations: as a great master, he understood the advantages of Legat's principles above the old ones.[53]

Legat himself recorded his approach to teaching, stating, "I opened my intuition, my ability to delve into the individuality of the dancers. . . . I saw the difference in their abilities. I precisely imagined in what poses, movements, groups and combinations I could show each to the best image, relying on their personal traits. I aspired to illuminate and underline their merits and conceal their inadequacies." Reflecting serenely, Legat concluded: "In this lies the secret of my success as a balletmaster. I was never an iconoclast or advocate of new forms. I was simply a searcher for wonderful individualism."[54]

In her memoir, Nina Tikanova commented that the sources of Legat's steps can still be found in the Royal Danish Ballet. Her lessons with Legat took place in Paris in the 1920s at a studio on the Rue des Petites-Écuries. She described his class as "difficult . . . it developed speed, not only in the legs, but in the mind," similar, perhaps, to Balanchine's approach to teaching. Tikanova observed that all of Legat's students "jumped well and had excellent batterie."[55] Legat changed his lesson daily in connection with whatever the focus of that class was and organized his lessons in advance. The barre work directly prepared the dancer for the adagio and the allegro to come, a method that would appear later in Vaganova's teaching. Blok wrote that Legat "knew the very core of movement, he precisely managed each individual. . . . If a young artist approached him before a performance in horror that he could not manage two *tours*, Legat would tell him exactly where to place the torso . . . and the *tours* would come."[56] His students included Nijinsky, Kshesinska, Trefilova, Karsavina, Vaganova, Yulia (Julie) Sedova, Fokine (before their stylistic parting of ways), and Adolph Bolm.

As her career continued, Vaganova was increasingly recognized for her dancing talents. Legat recalled her early days on the stage, a time "when any performance of Vaganova in the variations of her usual repertoire was accompanied by unanimous, stormy success. There was never a case when they didn't insist by means of persistent curtain calls that she repeat her variation, sometimes even twice."[57]

Vaganova as Kitri from the ballet *Don Quixote*, "a true ballerina's role."
Photo: Mariinsky Theatre Archives.

Vaganova danced *Swan Lake* for the first time on April 4, 1913, and again on October 30 of the same year. Reviewers called her the "queen of variations"; she was also referred to as the "martyr of ballet" and the "priestess of classical dance."[58] Indeed, more than once critics would remark that her jump was superior to Pavlova's:

> [Vaganova] darts from her place without a running start and hangs in the air, motionless, for several seconds. Her flight is even higher than Pavlova's ... but the art of Agrippina Vaganova is intertwined with inseparable virtuosity. Her dance is ... brilliant classical technique of a sort we haven't seen before on the stage of the Mariinsky Theatre.[59]

Ludmila Blok noted similarly that Vaganova's flight was "even higher than Pavlova's; thus the steps that were typically difficult for women, such as *cabriole avant*, suited her ideally, she beat her legs together high, like a man, executed it with all the strictness of classical requirements."[60]

Ballerina Alla Shelest, a 1937 graduate of the Leningrad Choreographic School, was known for her vibrancy and grace onstage, but also for the misfortunes that plagued her during her life—illness and breakdowns, and repeatedly being third or fourth cast despite her great technical and dramatic talents. She, too, commented on the quality of Vaganova's dancing, noting again her

> large jump, great aplomb, [she] wonderfully felt the sculpture of poses and movements, statically as well as dynamically. A determined beginning dominated the character of her dancing, a measured development of precision ... and a downplaying of the difficulties. It was these qualities that Agrippina Yakovlevna later cultivated in her own students. A person of great will, culture and anatomic intelligence, Vaganova worked very independently and fruitfully on perfecting the technique of classical dance, on its possibilities of expression.[61]

Nonetheless, endlessly demanding of herself, Vaganova sensed the insufficiencies of her dancing technique, and wrote, "It was obvious that I was not progressing. And that was a terrible thing to realize. So then I started to feel pangs of dissatisfaction both with myself and with the old system of teaching."[62]

Despite her growing successes, Vaganova's career on stage ended prematurely. Vaganova received the title of ballerina in 1915 at the age of thirty-six and retired from the stage just after the New Year. Initially she seemed to harbor no thoughts of dancing again. In her memoirs, she hinted at the complexity of this life transition away from the stage, writing cryptically that "the reasons weren't only due to the routine conditions of the Imperial stage." However, she was not offered a "benefice," or farewell gala concert, to celebrate her career, as was the usual practice for retiring ballerinas; instead she concocted one of her own. And, although officially retired, she signed a new contract with the theater from October 1, 1915, to January 1916 to dance four more ballets, and the farewell gala took place on January 10.

For her gala performance, Vaganova danced *La Source*, choosing to close her stage career with the same "big" ballet that had opened it. The role had won her praise in earlier years, and her success was repeated this time: critic Akim Volinsky wrote a long, detailed evaluation concluding with the declaration that throughout the evening, Vaganova's dancing "did not once fall below her own level of perfection. The public's ovations arose at the crescendo. After [she performed] Legnani's variation . . . the entire audience applauded, from the first to the last row. They applauded the talent [of Vaganova] at the peak of its strength, the phenomenal level of capability she had."[63]

On the day of her farewell concert, composer Alexander Glazunov himself sent Vaganova a telegram, congratulating her on the milestone. He wrote:

Recalling the first of your performances, [which were] linked with the time of my first brainchild ballet production, I welcome you and ask you to accept the expression of my sincere admiration and heartfelt gratitude.[64]

Of the composer's kind message, she recorded the following in her diary:

That telegram was a consolation to my grief, but a weak consolation. After all that I had lived to that point, everything was over. To lose art, to leave it, after all, is frightening. For me, a retired artist of the Imperial Theatres, nothing remains, aside from caring for the family. And that to me seems more bitter than death.[65]

Blok noted the indignation of the critics at the time, who found her retirement "at the prime of her talent" to be "pointless." But such was her fate. Then, as now, ballerinas did not typically dance beyond age forty. Fyodor Lopukhov commented on this phenomenon:

Along with appearance, slenderness, and the spiritual makeup of a dancer, one more, as I call it, frightening "addition" goes into the understanding of *emploi*—age. In choreography, age plays a specific role, as 40 years is the age of pension for the majority of dancers. But for a theatrical actor, it is his prime, and for the opera singer it is the most active age. While circus acrobats at 40 are already considered to be old.

And so, ballet, in terms of its relationship to age, stands almost next to the art of the circus—both there and here the execution depends in first order on the elasticity of the muscles and ligaments. I didn't want to write about this question—it is the most "explosive" [issue] for dancers, especially for females, but I understand that if I don't state my opinion, my articles such as *Choreographic Openness* will lose all of their meaning. However, in advance, I can see the indignation which will come across the ballerinas' brows, lending them the appearance of . . . a tigress, ready to pounce on me for one singular reminder of age. What can be done, I have to endure it."[66]

Following Vaganova's stage success at her farewell performance, there was a stage failure later that year. Officially retired, she danced an unsuccessful performance of *Giselle* in October 1915 while still on partial contract with the theater. It was a performance in which her technique was beyond reproach; nonetheless, "an airy, illusory, defenseless Giselle it was not."[67] Gaevsky argued insightfully that the romantic myth was not natural for her ("her very existence contradicted spectral phantasms, there was nothing illusory about her art") and that perhaps she was consciously making a statement against abstraction in this supposed performance "failure."[68]

Vaganova would dance again on the Mariinsky stage some years later, in 1922, on the occasion of completing twenty years of service in the theater. Her students also performed that evening, and one of them, the famous ballerina Marina Semënova, later wrote:

That night she danced the Grand Pas from *Paquita* and I fell in love with her brilliant tours and sharp, strong *cabrioles*. She was very musical. All her movements were connected to the music, always completed, always done as should be. In dance her technique, no matter how high [a level] it was, did not serve its own goal. Her dance was distinguished by full convergence with the music and was completely refined. Such brilliance, such certainty as Vaganova had, was not found at that time in the dancers we saw daily onstage. It seemed she was in full luster, full strength, and we ourselves saw confirmation of her talent. I had the feeling it wasn't the end, but just the beginning of something meaningful.[69]

Semënova's comments supported the critics' earlier lament over Vaganova's premature retirement. Unfortunately, despite her brilliant performance, the evening solidified Vaganova's decision that a stage career was not for her, a conclusion she explained in her diary:

But the break in the dancer's career and the fear of several ballerinas that I was again returning to the stages, convinced me to leave, conclusively and without looking back, all of the stage intrigues that were always so difficult for me.[70]

Her decision, along with the events of the October Revolution, were apparently impetus enough to lead her on a pedagogical journey that would change Russian ballet forever.

2

~

Vaganova the Teacher

Vaganova could have left Russia, as Preobrajenska and others did around the time of the Russian Revolution. Some left for political reasons; others saw no future for ballet in Russia or did not want to change the School program or the teaching system. But Vaganova remained behind, along with those in the intelligentsia who accepted the revolution and believed in Russia's Communist future. She felt that staying was necessary not only to preserve classical dance and ballet but also to propagandize this great art to the masses, to make it accessible and understandable to the new post-revolutionary spectator.[1]

If Petipa was part of the nineteenth century, Vaganova was part of the twentieth. Her teaching method took shape during the 1920s, a challenging time in the newly founded Soviet Union that tested the classical heritage of ballet. As the country shunned its Imperial past, the Ballet School was accused of "deliberate conservatism, backwardness, creative impotence; the critics demanded its reform 'from top to bottom.'"[2] The new left-wing press called ballet a hothouse art, conditioned by feudalism and doomed to perish under the new regime.

Konstantin Sergeyev, the illustrious Kirov Ballet dancer famous for his partnership with Natalia Dudinskaya, and subsequently the Kirov's artistic director, felt that the generation of ballet dancers that flourished during the 1920s and 1930s were the founding members of the Soviet ballet. He called it "a period of active, unforgettable volume of the Leningrad ballet" and explained,

> We were raised, grew up and matured during a difficult time of searching and experiments, of arguments "for" and "against" ballet theatre, and classical dance as its basis. . . . It was a time when the old world collapsed, the struggle against routine . . . disappeared, in which the stage of the Imperial Theatre became overgrown, a time of searches on the path of the unknown in the virgin soil of Soviet art. Sharp arguments boiled around ballet, which its enemies called "hotbed art," "hothouse growths," socially alien to the Soviet viewer, museum art, swept away by the revolution. Danger hung on the high culture of classical dance.

He further noted:

> It is by this restless period that the civil and ideological position of Vaganova, which she defended as much in theory as in practice, is defined. In the struggle with this barren, formalistic trend, nihilism and dilettantism also appeared, crystallizing Vaganova's method, defining her relationship to classical dance as the foundation of ballet theatre.[3]

Following her retirement from the stage, Vaganova's path to teaching at the Leningrad Choreographic School was not quite as direct as one might think. Her diary explains:

> In ballet, the pedagogues after the revolution included [Vera] Trefilova, [and] in the school only a part of its former workers remained, Zhukova and Preobrajenska [who left soon after, in 1921]. They also invited Zinaida Frolova and some of the artists, Mikhail Romanov, Evgenia Snetkova. No one invited me, so I taught at Baltflot and in Yuri Miklos' School as it was called, because Miklos was its director. Quite awful in many, if not in all respects. . . . But then Trefilova disappeared from the horizon (she emigrated to France). They invited me to work with the artists. Incidentally I received an

invitation to work with the younger classes of the school. With passion I accepted the work. The children were charming.[4]

Vaganova began her teaching career at the Leningrad Choreographic School with "a great love for the school . . . a love which no one could stop."[5] Andrey Oblakov was the director of the School at the time, and he hired her because he knew about her "desire, her irreproachable professionalism, and he unmistakenly guessed at her pedagogical calling."[6]

Though her installment at the School marked the beginning of her pedagogical work, Vaganova did not come to her position empty-handed. Her expertise, achieved by her own clever verification of each approach to movement or steps on herself, in her own dancing, could finally be made accessible to her students. The School needed a wise pedagogue who understood the responsibility of "standing in front of young Soviet ballet."[7] Furthermore, she had seriously thought about the "mechanics of the dancing body" and wanted to delve into the "secrets" of classical dance. Slonimsky observed that Vaganova's struggle with her own less-than-ideal physical traits was an important factor in her artistic development.[8] Indeed, as any aspiring dancer knows, overcoming physical inadequacies in ballet requires analytical thought and a creative approach to movement that leads to a deeper understanding of anatomy and human physiology. Nikolai Ivanovsky noted in the preface to Vaganova's published memoirs:

> Vaganova's method cannot be viewed separately from the life of the theatre. Not only because in the course of many years she was artistic director of the Leningrad Ballet, an irreplaceable pedagogue of the class of perfection for ballet soloists, but above all because she headed the modern school of female dancing mastery.[9]

A keen analysist, Vaganova kept an eye on her fellow dancers—and her instructors—throughout her years of training and performing. Her observations formed the base of her pedagogical method:

> Still, in her early youth Vaganova began to struggle with routine. Not coincidentally, the arms, the torso, the head attracted her attention. For these were the weakest places in the dance of the former generation of artists, and for Vaganova became the guide to expressive dance.

Agrippina Vaganova teaching class at the Leningrad Choreographic Institute. Photo: Mariinsky Theatre Archives.

She considered simplicity to be . . . wonderful, and achieved this simplicity, this harmonious freedom of the body, [and] mercilessly derided what blocked the path to it.[10]

Noting the strengths of both the Italian and French schools during her years of study, Vaganova was determined to assimilate them and impart her own observations when creating a single method of ballet training. Indeed her methodology was influenced by a long list of individuals. Her book, *Basic Principles of Classical Dance,* notes that her Russian predecessors—Anna Pavlova, Tamara Karsavina, Olga Preobrajenska—possessed a "poetic spirituality, a purely Russian 'cantilena' of movements, a wealth of expressive plastic nuances."[11] She tried to preserve these traits in her method. She also recalled Ekaterina Vazem's ability to develop both strength and softness in *plié,* and took that, along with Preobrajenska's elucidations of the Italian method as she began to construct her own system.

Vaganova also hoped to incorporate Fokine's natural *port de bras* and spirituality as she developed the Russian manner of dancing.[12] By "spirituality," one surmises that Blok refers to the stylized lyrical movements, the flowing grace of impressionism (as seen, for example, in *Chopiniana*) in contrast to the "droopiness" of the French school and the rigid, straight lines of the Italian school. In other words, a more harmonious movement incorporating only the best of French or Italian influences. We know from her achievements and published records that harmony of movement was one of Vaganova's main goals. She hoped to incorporate certain elements without catering to the trendy, modern movements of the time, such as those stemming from Isadora Duncan's influence. Renowned ballet historian and critic Vadim Gaevsky explains how, despite appearances and certain arguments, Vaganova did not return ballet theatre to the nineteenth century; rather, she pushed it ahead into the twentieth:

In any case, Fokine's "laissez-faire" freedom ended with Vaganova. And again the unquestionable academism became firmly established, free from everything that had been introduced into classical dance, the trendy "modern style," direct imitations of Isadora Duncan, and the more general inclination to the culture of impressionism. Vaganova eliminated the eclectic and reconstituted the canon, again drawing the pure line of classical dance. It seemed that she returned the ballet theatre to the nineteenth century. In that, the restoration of the archaic page, they blamed her heatedly. But it wasn't the case. In the classroom, Vaganova completely crystallized the new canon that she demonstrated in theatre work.[13]

Vaganova would crystallize the canon by emphasizing classical technique, developing and codifying it in the first established Russian system of ballet training. But that system would be adaptable, adjustable to the developments of the time, whether in terms of politics or in movement style.

Preobrajenska's relationship to her students is another vital component of pedagogy that Vaganova managed to replicate. Both women received immense reverence and respect from their students, and both created some of the most famous names on the ballet stage: "It was clear that Olga Osipovna [Preobrajenska] and her students respected one another. There were no shades of vulgarity in her, her irony was never insulting."[14] "Her lessons developed strength and elasticity of muscles, developed endurance, gave difficult combinations. She never sat on the chair during the lesson. She never lifted her voice or screamed at the children."[15]

Equipped then, with her own observations of pedagogues such as Preobrajenska and Fokine, and shifting away, slightly, from the previous trends in "classical" *port de bras*, Vaganova set out to revamp and institutionalize the entire code of ballet schooling. Through her work, she developed an understanding of the correct coordination of the body.[16] Her method did not focus on the arms or legs in isolation, however. Rather it incorporated, for the first time, the idea that the entire body should be involved in the movement, and that *port de bras* and the basics of technique would aid in the overall coordination of steps and jumps:

> Vaganova considered the firm training of the torso to be the major prerequisite of free bodily control in dancing. From the first *pliés*, which she recommended be learned from 1st position, which is more difficult for beginners but important for strengthening the body, her efforts were directed at the development of aplomb. This

aplomb later on becomes the foundation for tours and difficult allegro jumps.[17]

In her book, *Basic Principles of Classical Dance*, Vaganova frequently underlines that movement must begin "from the [whole] body," which allows the desired bearing, and artistic decoration of steps. Special attention is paid to *épaulement*, or the inclination of the shoulders, torso, and head. Variety of steps was also a clear focus: in her lessons, Vaganova did not permit or promote having two steps in a row that used the same position of the body. Having developed the necessary stability and flexibility in her students, she then introduced more complicated steps into their dance vocabulary, such as *fouetté, renversé*, and other movements that are based on the inclination of the torso.[18] Finally, she instilled a conscious approach to movement, an analytical line of attack that was unique at the time. Vaganova's pupils not only mastered steps, they could also explain how to perform them correctly and what their purpose was.[19] Ballerina Alla Shelest recalled this new, unique approach in ballet:

> We related to Agrippina Yakovlevna with full trust, any of her remarks were absolutely precise and usually fulfilled without compromise. She insisted that we do everything consciously, trained us to analyze other executions, to find mistakes in ourselves and in our classmates. Sometimes she would stop class and we had to explain the reason for the failure, and show how to correct it. Vaganova imparted in us the ability to go deeply into the image of this or that movement, to understand what the work of the torso and arms serve, "the decoration of movement"—the length of arabesque, perfection of attitude, the stability of turns—in a word, she taught us to give meaning to dance in all its harmony.
>
> Strict discipline in the lessons—and here, benevolence, respect for talent, for self-sufficiency and initiative—these were very important traits to Vaganova the teacher.[20]

In addition to the focus on dance "with the whole body," a new *port de bras*, harmony of movement, and a new analytical approach to successful step sequences, the features of Vaganova's method also included a rigorous planning of the teaching process, which one can surmise was modeled in part after Cecchetti's regimented lessons. Similar to Legat, who carefully prepared his lessons, Cecchetti had a fixed lesson plan for each class, which had helped cultivate his following.[21] While Vaganova found the Italian movements to be alternately overly angular and too straightened, especially in the case of *port de bras*—she would later refer to the awkward "straight" position of the upright spine in *attitude croisé* and *effacé* in her textbook and criticize the unstretched knees in arabesque and in *changements de pied* of the Italian school—the idea of well-prepared lessons appealed to her. She would add her own touch to Legat's model; veering away from the unalterable lesson plan of her own teacher Johansson, she would shift the content of her classes based on the students' needs.

Her student Marina Semënova recalled this element of Vaganova's lessons, which "appeared as if they were repetitious, but without fail something new appeared in them. She cultivated in us the unlimited possibility to master the body, a sense of strength, beauty, and of course musicality, and the flexibility of the dance in the body."[22] Blok noted the benefits of structured lesson plans and their impact on the student:

> Systematic lessons of uniform repetition imbed the lasting and mechanical adoption of correct execution, desired turnout, severity of form. [In contrast,] varied lessons, arousing the student's involuntary attention, [and] insisting that the student surmount the unexpected composition of steps and difficulties, supports a detailed array of the artistic condition. The student is active, works harder and achieves results more quickly. Vaganova is a hot supporter of the second method, and no one else has so excelled in the inventiveness and unexpected nature of her combinations, thus her lessons are so valued by her students.[23]

It sounds almost paradoxical: under Vaganova, instead of simple static drills, exercises were given in various combinations, while the execution of the poses and steps themselves had to be done in a singular manner. In this way the dance became more colorful, and the students' minds were kept alive while they coped with new approaches to a variety of step combinations, to a diverse choreography within each lesson. Further, the participation of the students in the lesson—requiring their own critique

Agrippina Vaganova in 1935. The previous year she published her textbook, *Basic Principles of Classical Dance,* and received the prestigious title "People's Artist of the USSR." Photo: Mariinsky Theatre Archives.

and analysis of movement, body placement, and the process of trial and error—effectively gave Vaganova's pupils more than just a knowledge of specific ballet steps: she involved their analytical minds, inculcating her own approach to movement in those who would later be her successors. This contrasts with the "decorated" style of dance so embraced by the French. As Blok, who often observed Vaganova's lessons, explained:

> Solidity, compactness, "three-dimensionality" lie at the core of her students' technique. This is far from being painted on the flatness of poorly drawn decorative vignettes, it is far from naturalistic plastique. Her students' technique is closest of all to a modern sense of architecture. The architecture of movement, where all is thought out in advance, all is a complete whole, solid, reliable, and economical. You won't see anything decorative in Vaganova's lesson, nothing shown for pleasure at a given moment. . . . All of the movement leads to one goal.[24]

Blok noted that the "formerly swaying and uncoordinated form of dance" of the 1910s that preceded Vaganova was completely eliminated with Vaganova's entry into the world of pedagogy. "Now it is clear at first glance to any attentive spectator that we are dealing with a uniform, solitary technique of dance for the entire troupe, that the type of dance of the Leningrad Ballet in 1937 is truly the work of Vaganova's hands, it is Vaganova's style."

That single phrase, "Vaganova style," is now known the world over and represents a specific kind of ballet, a specific technique and way of moving. At the time, Blok called it "strong, bright optimism and dance realism, nothing 'otherworldly' or inappropriate, only pleasing to the eye;" she continued:

> Each of her poses is constructive . . . with a sober, business approach to movement, built on the play of muscles and consciously leading them into a new order of compactness, steadfastness, three-dimensionality, [this] lies at the basis of her students' technique. This is far from coloring a flat plane, or even sculpture, "human, too human." The technique of Vaganova's students is closest of all to modern construction. Construction in movement—all is thought out, all is sensible, definite, reliable and firm.[25]

Nikolai Ivanovsky, director of the Ballet School from 1940 to 1952, explained how Vaganova's innate pedagogical eye was constantly evolving:

Vaganova's lesson was always thought out on all sides. . . . She came to class firmly knowing what needed to be given to the students that day. Always connected with their lives, she knew the level of fatigue-ability, and the workload of each class [year]. Thus her lessons never overworked [the students], and didn't allow the students to slack off, or to "spare themselves" as she loved to say.

Cultivating ever-new cadres, Vaganova intermittently expanded herself; not stopping the search for the new in art, the pedagogue perfected her method, made the lessons and the technique of her students more difficult. Very often she asked a student to write a difficult combination down for the next lesson, an adagio or allegro, sometimes an entire lesson . . . she wanted to force the students to think, to understand the meaning of this or that movement. She awakened their creative imagination and taught them to independently correct the execution of each step.[26]

Urging the students to analyze movement was Vaganova's means of incorporating a more intellectual or even scientific approach to movement, and one that had not, to date, been widespread. It is noteworthy that Agrippina Yakovlevna demanded the same devotion to continuous growth in her students that she asked of herself.

The benefits of Vaganova's training system reached not only the women who studied ballet but the men as well. According to Blok:

Now in the Leningrad Ballet we are experiencing an epoch of bright decoration, carrying an eternal, distinct style of execution, an epoch which is inseparably connected to the name of Vaganova. Not only female dance, the dance of the direct students of Vaganova, but also the male dance personifies the manner and style of this great artist. Vaganova was as sharply modern in dance as she is an uncompromising realist. . . . [S]he deeply and intuitively sensed the laws of movement and how they are construed.[27]

Former Kirov Ballet dancer Pyotr Gusev, who later directed the ballet company in Novosibirsk, spoke reverently of Vaganova's legacy in 1958:

In just under 40 years, Vaganova graduated several hundred dancers from the Leningrad Choreographic Institute. Among them were those with amazing capabilities and those without any aptitude for dance. But no matter what the level of the student's capabilities, even the most unlucky of them knew the technology of classical dance in full volume. . . . The school and method of Vaganova even to this day is the leader of Soviet ballet pedagogy, and supports its student-pedagogues. . . . Her life should not be considered other than a heroic feat. The work of a ballet pedagogue is thankless. It is unnerving and intensive, requiring that talent, as a rule, remain in the shadows. The successes of a student bring great joy, but more often the teacher's share brings grief, for the student usually forgets that they owe their success to their teacher. Even Vaganova survived more than a few severe disappointments. But there is no doubt that the generation of Soviet ballet, both this one and the next one, will be proud of Vaganova—a great pedagogue of the Soviet Choreographic Art.[28]

Konstantin Sergeyev also attested to the influence of Vaganova's new technique in the realm of male dancing:

Vaganova did not forgive the smallest inexactitude, did not indulge or make any concessions. On the contrary, the value of a great physical load, of the maximum mobilization of the psyche allowed an authentic freedom to involuntarily pour out [of the dancer] in accordance with movements which made the dance unique. Learning the difficulty of Vaganova's grammar of classical dance, I tried to apply it in my classes and rehearsals. Male dance acquired great strictness, completeness of form and expression due to the coordination of movements of the arms and torso, softening the strong method needed for jumps and turns.[29]

Blok and Ivanovsky, of course, observed Vaganova's "style" as far back as the 1930s and 1940s. That style is still recognized as representing the technique and manner of movement that Vaganova codified.

Individuality

By all accounts, Vaganova was a dancer with unique dancing talents. But she did not attempt to replicate her own dancing traits in her students; she did not aim to create carbon copies of herself. Blok observed this phenomenon:

> However, equipped with the shining technique of her students, Agrippina Yakovlevna—unfortunately this must be said—has not given her high style of dancing to anyone else, the dance of Vaganova-the-ballerina. And when we speak of "Vaganova's" manner, we speak of Vaganova-the-pedagogue, of the style of her students and not of her own time as a dancer.
>
> . . . Vaganova's dance, given to her students, is broken into as many individual manners as there were talented individuals among her students. Each took it in their own way.[30]

Fyodor Lopukhov made a similar observation:

> In the rush to "create" out of their students "a ballerina" and a "premiere danseur," and in the flurry of their massive preparations, thoughts about individual physical build have diminished. Incidentally, neither Legat nor Vaganova ever flaunted the phrase "my student." I, at least, never heard anything of the kind from their mouths.[31]

For a number of reasons, the issue of individuality must be recognized as a crucial part of Vaganova's pedagogical system. Her work attempted to unify training under her new pedagogical system. Despite the political atmosphere that deemphasized the individual in favor of the collective and wanted the arts to promulgate that value, she did not aim to obliterate individuality in dancers. Support for *emploi*, the practice of typecasting dancers into certain roles—ballerina, soubrette, lyrical dancer—and then forbidding crossover into ballets outside the dancer's defined "type" stemmed from the Imperial era. In cultivating her teaching system, however, Vaganova met the Soviet demands for a revised ballet School. Her focus was more flexible than the tracking scheme inherent in *emploi*: she aimed to create a system by which dancers could train in a single, unified style that gives breath, emotion, and life to the dance. Those who studied

Agrippina Vaganova with her students in the studios of the Choreographic Institute, later renamed the Vaganova Academy in her honor. Photo: Mariinsky
Theatre Archives.

under her might argue that this unification meant a loss of individuality.
Indeed in some respects that is true: one cannot maintain synchrony in a
corps de ballet when each dancer is attempting to stand out of the crowd.
But at the time, Vaganova went not in search of fame or reward for creating this or that ballerina; her goal was not to create a ballet "star" but to
codify and establish a singular Russian method of dancing. She managed
to do so without suppressing individual students' talents.

In 1937, Lopukhov offered a dissenting opinion on Vaganova's approach to *emploi*, relating it to the farewell concert in which she danced
part of *Giselle*:

> I have difficulty saying exactly when the disdainful relationship to
> *emploi* began. I allow that it was with the farewell gala concert of
> Vaganova, when she danced *Giselle*, contradicting her artistic traits.

Ever since, the denial of *emploi* has risen, because *Vaganova ignored this understanding and tried to make her students versatile dancers, capable of fulfilling any role.* But a person capable of dancing everything has not been born yet and never will be born. It is high time to put an end to the disdainful relationship to *emploi*, which at present predominates in our ballet theatres.[32]

This development of unified synchronicity may be seen as a reflection of the Soviet political climate of the 1930s. When a society's ideology demands uniformity, equality, and the submission of the self to the betterment of the communal whole, regardless of individuality or talent, the goal of group synchronicity would seem at first glance to fit well politically. However, we would be remiss to view Vaganova's achievements as entirely politically motivated. The art of ballet, then as now, provides the ultimate example of individualism: the ballerina, the princess, the loveliest girl in the precinct, whether it is a forest, a village, or a lakeside full of swans. Even in the Soviet Union, talented individuals were rewarded for their contributions to the state, and selected as examples for others. In this way, Vaganova's creation of a codified system of training, a single method and "look" for the ballet dancers, bears less of a relationship to the politics of the 1930s than to the requirements for an organized, complex basis upon which Russia's historically aristocratic art form could further expand and grow. In fact, her method cultivated individual ballerina personalities as well as a uniform, identically trained *corps de ballet.* Her efforts are evident even today in the Mariinsky's esteemed *corps de ballet*, a sea of well-trained, academic dancers who take their art seriously. And among Vaganova's own students we see a wide range of dancer-types with talents in different aspects of dance. Marina Semënova, Galina Ulanova, Feya Balabina, Natalia Dudinskaya—each is completely different from the next. Moreover, Vaganova continued to coach these ballerinas as they began their professional careers. It is she, for example, who worked with Ulanova on her debut as Odette/Odile, and with Tatiana Vecheslova in *The Red Poppy*, after the budding ballerinas had left the School.

In fact, many of Vaganova's contemporaries observed her ability to cultivate individuality in her students. Among them was Lidia Evmentieva, a dancer trained by Vaganova and a teacher herself:

It is surprising how vigilantly Vaganova was able to see each dancer, her individual traits, the qualities inherent only in her, the potential possibilities and inadequacies. She helped develop one and correct the other. Just as a jeweler working on a valuable stone is compelled to play with all of its facets, in this way identifying its essence, so Vaganova added luster and sharpened talent. The young ballet dancers, making only their first steps in art, with her help quickly found their talent, and were eternally grateful. It should be specifically emphasized that Vaganova never thrust her own individuality on anyone. All of her students had strict classical training, distinguished by a single school—the Vaganova school—but all were surprisingly different by the character of their artistic handwriting. In each of them she sees and [further] reveals their individuality.[33]

Supporter of Reform: The 1920s

In 1926 Vaganova wrote about the path of ballet in her diary:

Of course the ballet repertoire has seriously aged. It is necessary to renew, to freshen the relationship with the spirit of the time. Now when new life appears in the ballet troupe, automatically the question arises: can this young dancer who has gone through the "old" classical school with its methods of teaching, work in the conditions of revolutionized ballet subjects, dance, and be not just passive inert material, but actively participate in new work? I stand on the point of view that classical ballet such as this will not die. It is the basis, the school upon which anything new can be built. Now it is still hard to foresee the path of the new ballet, the evolution of the ballet subject and its formation in dance, but it seems to me that in revolutionary ballet, the role of the separate artists cannot be reduced to "no." The ballet performance always—past, present and future—must develop separate facts, ideas, entire events in front of the viewer . . . to give the full allegory of conventionality, and even of fairytales. Thus the individual artist with his talent can symbolize defined ideas or entire events (for example, Freedom, and so on.)[34]

She claims that the foundation of ballet is classical technique, but she also recognizes the need to move forward. At the outset of Vaganova's teaching career, the ongoing war between those who supported far-reaching reform in ballet and those who wished to preserve the traditions of classical dance was cause for significant concern. This debate was in many ways an outlet for Russia's struggling nationalism: the desire to distinguish Russia's dance tradition from its French or Italian predecessors, to codify something of its own, to welcome the new, but not completely reject the classical heritage. The anxiety in the post-Revolution years that national treasures were being corrupted could no longer be directed toward foreigners. By the 1920s, the search for the "new" took place entirely within Russia's well of homegrown artistic talent, and in Soviet-era dance, the struggle both for and against novelty took place among choreographers, artistic directors, and innovators.

Despite the revolutionary nature of her unique, solidified pedagogical system, Vaganova belonged to the classical camp. She recognized that ballet—like any form of art—would change with the times. She did not aim to destroy classical tradition, but codify and develop it.

The shifts that characterized Russian art, including ballet, in the 1920s included the growing rejection of anything that smacked of aristocratic, elite life. Ballet fell into that category, as previously noted. Despite Vaganova's efforts to help build a pedagogical method, and in spite of her adherence to some of the norms of the era, she did not accept all of the models promulgated during those years. Critic Vadim Gaevsky noted that Vaganova aspired to structure and clear language, adopting the developments of physical form from the 1920s, while rejecting the passionless psychological models of those years, which were above emotion. He described the formula for her school, which he deemed clearly neoclassical, as emotionally expansive with an absolutely reserved "plasticheski" physical form, the emblem of which is her Diana and Acteon pas de deux.[35]

What were those passionless psychological models? Soviet ballet of the 1920s was heavily influenced by the politics of the time. Pavel Petrov's Solveig, a Norwegian love story that premiered on September 24, 1922, was criticized for lacking unity and being composed of "separate dances, scenes, and groups, totally unconnected, sometimes even contradictory."[36] Likewise, Alexander Gorsky's *Ever-Fresh Flowers* (1922), a revolutionary children's ballet that made use of Soviet pageantry, promoted the idea of the proletariat, even encouraging audience participation, and thereby revealed the problem of trying to combine a propagandist political agenda and high art.[37] The better-known *The Red Poppy* (1927), which centered on the awakening of class consciousness among Chinese revolutionaries, had an abundance of pantomime and provoked hot debate.[38] Lopukhov's own production of *The Red Whirlwind* (1924) attempted to show the "birth of socialism, the dawn and development of the revolution, its struggle with counterrevolution, and the birth and affirmation of communism."[39] In fact, according to Elizabeth Souritz, his choice of movements "led to an impoverishment of the lexicon, an imitation of gymnastics, which many at that time used in opposition to 'outdated' classicism."[40] If nothing else, the 1920s in Russian ballet reflected the athletic, youthful ideal, sometimes acrobatic, and closely tied to the country's politics. "The ballets created then about modern events and about the revolution proved to be far from the most modern and revolutionary," Souritz wrote. "Addressing Soviet reality and telling of popular uprisings, the choreographers encountered problems so complex that this is where there were [the] most mistakes and least success."[41] Gaevsky wrote of Vaganova:

> For this reason her students so easily entered the best productions of *dramballet* and for this reason they were able to dance leading roles in the old, emotionally saturated repertoire. They danced these roles in a new way, free from the conventions of the French school that had been preserved since the time of Petipa. And even during Petipa's time, Vaganova turned out to be a dancer who disrupted the bases of this French school. The aesthetic of grace was alien to her: Petipa noticed it first.[42]

However, Gaevsky referred to grace in the soft, feminine sense of the word, a quality that stands in opposition to Vaganova's strong jumps and bravura manner of dancing which some have referred to as "masculine." Vaganova's system itself, and not her personal performing style, cultivated harmony of movement, beautiful lines, and consistent poses—as such, it can be described as graceful.

When Fyodor Lopukhov was appointed artistic director of the State

Academic Theatre of Opera and Ballet in 1922, he staged a number of ballets that did not correspond to Vaganova's aesthetic views. Lopukhov was responsible for the first Soviet stagings of many critical works from the Petipa-Ivanov era, such as *The Sleeping Beauty* and *Raymonda*, and he was also one of the more avant-garde creators of "new art" in the Soviet era. Pyotr Gusev explained how Lopukhov's ballets presented classical dance that was "very limited with its numerous acrobatic ways. In solos, the ballerina did splits, cartwheels, squat-dances, crawling, turned-in positions along with turned-out ones, sport-style jumps, et cetera, using many acrobatic methods until then unknown in ballet."[43] While introducing what Vaganova saw as "circus" tricks to ballet, Lopukhov, in his book *Writings on Ballet and Music*, defended classical ballet by discussing the necessity of symphonic dance, the need to use steps as a repetitive choreographic motif, to express certain musical characteristics, and not simply for the sake of filling up space. "I cannot be persuaded that the art of choreography, with classical dance at this pinnacle, is superfluous," he wrote.[44] "Classical dance is essentially classless and international and expresses otherworldliness and lightness of being. Choreography's most perfect form, the 'dance symphony,' is based upon classical dance. . . . I believe that the negative view of classical dance as being irrelevant to the new social order is largely a consequence of ignorance of the art and its potential and can therefore be easily overturned."[45]

In this, both Lopukhov and Vaganova seemed to share the same point of view, at least initially. Vaganova claimed that "whatever the elements are that go into classical ballet, dance, and exercises, they are the basis of the entire building of choreographic art."[46] At first she felt compelled to help the dancers cast in Lopukhov's ballets, proving that she could evaluate ballet even if it was based on principles she did not share. That occurred with Lopukhov's *Ice Maiden* in 1927. As Dudinskaya wrote, "When the production of a form of dance that was alien to her truly became a work of art, she didn't just announce it, she lauded it."[47] When Lopukhov was staging his works at the Mariinsky, Vaganova observed the students' struggle with his new athletic and acrobatic steps:

She saw how [her own student] Mungalova sought new means to warm up the body before rehearsals of Lopukhov's ballets. She understood that classical training was not enough to overcome technical difficulties of the acrobatic order. Glancing at Mungalova and other students, Vaganova unexpectedly came to their aid. She came to include elements of acrobatics and even separate dancing phrases from new performances in her lessons with artists from the Kirov Opera and Ballet Theatre.

This called forth various reactions: mockery and blame from some, surprise and gratitude from others, but most of all, confusion, lack of understanding and apprehension. Still, Vaganova, herself a stronghold of pure classical dancing, suddenly helps Lopukhov "destroy" what is holy! But Vaganova . . . simply could not avoid searching for a means to overcome the new challenges that were unexpectedly appearing; [challenges] which the good training on students' bodies turned out to be unprepared for after all.[48]

It is telling that Agrippina Yakovlevna assisted a choreographer whose essentially acrobatic movement she opposed in many ways. In a 1930s diary entry, she explained her decision to come to Lopukhov's aid:

Can we introduce physical training exercises and acrobatics on the stage when we encounter them first at the circus, and second at the Stadium or sports field? There can be only one answer: of course not. . . . We will achieve nothing new by bringing them to the stage *without the corresponding treatment.* This treatment itself, the polishing required for the stage, we can carry out only on the basis of the classical exercise. . . . Independent from the direction that the reforms of ballet take, the classical exercise must remain the foundation of theatre dance.[49]

However, Vaganova's support for Lopukhov was short-lived. Following Lopukhov's *The Nutcracker* in 1929, which provoked an outrage in the theater, Vaganova viewed his growing acrobatic tendencies as

an encroachment on what was sacred to her art. Until then she had remained impartial but now she joined the camp of Lopukhov's adversaries. She made fun of Lopukhov's *Nutcracker* with an innocent look on her face, dismissing it right away. However, it was not the right time to joke. Vaganova was seriously concerned that this fascination with acrobatics, which was beginning to take hold at the school . . . could pollute the purity of classical dance, which she was prepared to defend to the end. From year to year, while strengthening the reputation of her own classes, she was also concerned about the reputation of the Vocational School of Choreography, as it was now called.[50]

Krasovskaya pointed to Lopukhov's *Nutcracker* as the fateful mistake that first weakened his absolute authority in the theater, making way for Vaganova.[51] Given the strong political influences within the realm of art at the time, no one was above criticism. Critic Ivan Sollerinsky praised Lopukhov's desire to convey a factory production process through dance in his 1931 production of *Bolt* set to music by Shostakovich, but recognized the disconnectedness and inconsistency of the choreography with the symphonic music.[52] Yuri Slonimsky recognized Lopukhov's contributions to Soviet choreography by introducing important stylistic changes, changes that ultimately did not endure: "[he] helped prove to the new generation of the ballet that seeking form alone cannot promote the growth of choreography. Of the storms and trials of this period, the classical dance emerged victorious."[53]

Subsequently an avalanche of protest fell upon Lopukhov. Soon the press would suggest he be removed from his position as director and return to choreography.

It is important to note that Vaganova wasn't opposed to novel ways of moving; she was opposed to abandoning the classical foundation, or replacing it with something else. She maintained that classical ballet must continuously draw its source from classical training, and only then generate new forms of movement. Her initial attempt to create a basis of physical preparation that addressed the unique requirements of Lopukhov's choreography speaks to her analytical talents as a pedagogue and her broad-minded approach to her art. She attempted to participate in the development of ballet as an art form, while still preserving its foundations.

The Results of Her Efforts

Amid the criticism of the theatre School in the 1920s, the ongoing war between reformers and traditionalists, and the growing trend of socialist realism that would be officially promulgated by Stalin's decree of 1932,

Vaganova's first graduating students appeared: Olga Mungalova and Nina Mlodzinskaya (1923), and Natalia Kamkova and Elena Tangieva-Berzniek (1924). Soon Marina Semënova would astonish audiences with her expressive arms, strong turns, and overall virtuosity. In 1928 Galina Ulanova graduated, followed by Natalia Dudinskaya and Feya Balabina in 1931, both of whom later became outstanding ballerinas and leading pedagogues. Balabina was to train a class of male dancers that included Gennadi Seliutskiï, who danced with Rudolf Nureyev and today teaches and coaches at both the Mariinsky Theatre and the Vaganova Academy. Thus the seeds of Vaganova's efforts blossomed into dancers of national, and later, international renown as the first generation of Soviet ballet artists trained by Vaganova herself.

It is telling that the first generation of Vaganova's "ballerinas" coincided with her own appointment as artistic director of the Kirov Ballet in 1931. She would retain the post until 1937, when politics would necessitate directing her energies exclusively to the School. Her views did not coincide with those of the young balletmasters of the time, and the Committee for Artistic Affairs under the Soviet of People's Commissars USSR supported the newer tendencies in art. Nonetheless, during her six-year directorship of the company, the change in the company's dancing quality was noted by many. Blok wrote, "As a result of her directorship, the uncoordinated manner of dance of the previous decade was completely eliminated, and now from first glance it becomes clear to any attentive viewer that we are dealing with a unified, solitary technique of dance in the whole troupe."[54]

On the anniversary of what would have been Vaganova's one-hundredth birthday, numerous articles lauding the great pedagogue and her contributions to Russian art appeared in the Russian press. Konstantin Sergeyev, a former premier danseur and artistic director of the Kirov Ballet, wrote of her gifts:

> Vaganova's reforms in the area of classical dance are based above all on the results of her own artistic experience. A brilliant dancer of the former Mariinsky Theatre, she tested and believed in her own worth and in the inadequacies of two supremacies at the time in the Petersburg school: the French, with its sluggish movements and sugary manner, and the Italian, cultivating virtuosity,

the dynamic of dance, which was accompanied by a harshness and did not deliver poetry. Vaganova saw the advantages of a Russian national school of dance with its poetic spirituality and cantilena of movement. But the Russian school of classical dance wasn't yet strengthened in pedagogical practice, and needed perfecting and modernization.

Vaganova combined the achievements of Russian and foreign dancers, balletmasters and teachers at the end of the 19th, beginning of the 20th century. Developing her Soviet method, she defined the new qualities of execution for female dancing and rendered an indubitable influence on the development of male dancing. Two aspects eternally stand out to me in this method. Developing the best characteristics of the features of the Russian school, Vaganova brought in the correct carriage of the torso and spine, which gave absolute freedom of expression and an exact coordination of all parts of the body which as a result acquire expression and plastique in flight. Agrippina Yakovlevna taught all movements "from the torso." This dance advantageously distinguishes Russian ballets from foreign ones. Vaganova's demand to dance not only with the legs, but also with the arms and torso, opened up new possibilities for mastery of the lexicon of modern classical dance, which defined the inimitable Leningrad Ballet School.

A second and no less important contribution is [her treatment of] the arms, not only when expressing the conclusion of each movement, but in actively helping during jumps and various turns. Beautiful, strong, energetic arms defined the strong-willed character of the dance, setting the basis for the heroic characters in Soviet ballet.

Vaganova gave great meaning to a wide range of movements, demanding their modern elegance and absolute harmony with the music.[55]

Sergeyev explained how the young generation of Soviet dancers did not want to be "locked up in the framework of the wonderful past of Russian ballet. Vaganova actively took young dancers from the side, became their ideologue, supported their artistic enthusiasm, searching for artists and ballet masters, [and] welcomed such landmark performances as Vasily Vainonen's *The Flames of Paris* (1932) and *Partisans Days* (1937); Rostislav Zakaharov's *Lost Illusions* (1936) and *The Fountain of Bachchisarai* (1934); and Leonid Lavrovsky's *Fadetta* (1936)."[56]

The 1930s and Dramballet

In 1925, Elizaveta Gerdt, a leading ballerina in the theater, claimed that the "old ballets with their ... pompous triviality ... can no longer satisfy the modern viewer." Along with her, Leonid Leontiev, a balletmaster at the School, declared that the creation of "new forms, more understandable to the modern viewer" were necessary.[57] This heated debate continued into the 1930s in the newspapers and within the theater regarding the state of ballet in the new Soviet Russia.

The Great October Revolution had created a new audience. Classical ballet was seen as elitist and tainted with the values of the aristocracy and bourgeoisie. Something had to replace it. Vaganova's new pedagogical system was slowly adopted in the School. But changes also needed to be made on the stage. The first step was to revise the ballet repertoire, to "renew" or revise the old classical warhorses in order to make them "understandable" to the modern, Soviet viewer. This revisionist trend had begun in the 1920s, continued into the 1930s, and now Vaganova would directly participate in it.

Vaganova began to work on revising the ballet productions, infusing them with a new look and approach. Along with composer Boris Asafiev, the in-house musical adviser at the time, stage producer Sergei Radlov, conductor Evgenii Mravinsky, and scenarist and dancer Vladimir Dmitriev, Vaganova revised the previous version of *Swan Lake* while "maximally adhering to Tchaikovsky's composition, freeing it from many of the naïvetés of the fairytale subject, of the phony heap of pantomime scenes with relative gestures translated into the psychological sphere."[58] Vaganova herself wrote that it was necessary to avoid the "templated" or standardized, ages-old pantomime scenes that were, at the time "poorly understood and alien to the modern viewer."[59] The basic task of the new production, she wrote, is "to avoid unnecessary conventionality and make a ballet [that is] more available to the mass viewer." She elaborates in her diary:

Moments of "danced" pantomime, if you can call them that, [and] mysticism are deleted. The stereotyped "peasant" is excluded from the waltz in the first scene. . . . I think I acted correctly when, to the tempo of a Polonaise I set a sextet and not an evening waltz in that scene. The well-built apotheosis, recalling "a village paradise" has been replaced by the tragic ending of an unsuccessful romance.[60]

The revised *Swan Lake* was transformed into the story of a young count captive of his own romantic illusions. He pursues a swan at the lake who represents eternal youthful femininity. The dream of his ideal prevents his marriage to a neighboring landlord's daughter, leading to his ultimate destruction.[61] Vaganova eliminated Odette's pantomime in her initial encounter with the Prince in order to tighten the dramatic flow; she introduced new variations in both the second and third acts, and restored parts of the score that had previously been cut.[62]

In her book, *Zapiski Balerini* (*Notes of a Ballerina*), Vaganova graduate and pedagogue Lidia Evmentieva wrote about Vaganova's efforts in this ballet:

At the foundation of Agrippina Yakovlevna Vaganova's version lies the attempt at a concrete, emotional substantiation of images, in contrast to the magical fairytale-like dramaturgy of the first version. Vaganova didn't change the dramatic character of the libretto which is definitively connected to the music. The poetic fairytale . . . received a new treatment: . . . Vaganova treated the image of the Swan as a rebirth of the youth's fantasy. . . . Siegfried's image becomes concrete and emotional in her production.[63]

Natalia Dudinskaya later recalled the modernity of Vaganova's modern approach to these revisions:

Agrippina Yakovlevna was not conservative. On the contrary, she keenly felt the pulse of time, and walked [forward] from the epoch in which she lived. This further explains her balletmaster's activity. Remaining the guardian of classical dance, she thought Petipa's ballets glorified the pre-revolutionary Imperial Theatre, and could not be understood by the modern viewer in all of their components. A different epoch, different people, different requirements.

Along with the great dancers, the masterpieces of Petipa in these ballets, there is lots of pantomime, purely relative gestures that are understood only by the ballet dancer, and Agrippina Yakovlevna looked over *Swan Lake* and *Esmeralda* from the position of modern demands.[64]

Indeed, the undertaking was a risky one: editing Ivanov and Petipa meant preserving the classical heritage, which her diary entries acknowledge. The extent to which she actually did so, however, is questionable.

At the premiere, audience reaction was sharply divided. Those who defended tradition saw no reason to revise the heritage of the great masters, while supporters of the new staging thought the ballet's authors conveyed the emotional content of the music while successfully avoiding explanations of the plot and too much symbolism.[65]

Ballerina Alla Shelest noted Vaganova's permanent influence on what we now perceive as standard technique in this ballet:

Vaganova conceived of the wrists in the swan acts. She easily modified the strict classical form, however without the impurities of breaking expression and line. These arms turned out to be so musical that now you cannot even imagine "Swan Lake" without them. Irreproachable tact and a sense of the modern allowed her to insert a correction of the stylistically accurate movement that many representatives from the current generation of balletmasters and dancers cannot distinguish from the choreography of Lev Ivanov and Marius Petipa. As a point of fact, Vaganova's creative search turned out to be the riverbed of the direction of development of Soviet art—its aspiration to realistic methods and to stage truth.[66]

Irina Trofimova, who studied with Vaganova, still teaches at the Vaganova Academy today. A fragile, gentle woman with a sharp memory despite her age, Trofimova was a member of the last graduating class of pedagogues that Vaganova taught at the Rimsky-Korsakov Conservatory before her death. Irina's treasure trove of experiences and memories from the Soviet years has never before been recorded in print. One hot summer day I joined her at her dacha located several hours outside of Petersburg.[67] Instead of being fearful or cold to a foreigner, she was happy to discuss her life experience, and would pause to consider a question,

Irina Trofimova, present day, with her students inside the Vaganova Academy studios. Trofimova is one of few pedagogues who was trained by Vaganova herself and still teaches at the Academy. Photo courtesy of the Vaganova Academy.

or embark on a sudden tangent to recall the steps and hum the melodies from a long-lost ballet. Trofimova explains that, before Vaganova, the use of the arms in *Swan Lake* was nothing like we see today:

> Vaganova, through her method, provided dancers with the mastery of the whole body that easily facilitates the incorporation of soul and emotion and thoughts about the characterization. She always worked a lot on the flexibility, on the "conversation" of the spine and back. She worked on wrists a great deal. Earlier, only the elbows in ballet moved, but Vaganova incorporated the wrists also. In *Swan Lake* the *port de bras* are hers, and they fit the image of the swan perfectly. This was part of her talent.

Along with the restaging of old productions, Soviet ballet of the 1930s was characterized by the influence of drama on new choreography. The official requirements of socialist realism and the demand for audience accessibility led to the dominance of this genre in art of all kinds. The so-called *dramballet* appeared, consisting of multiple-act productions most often based on classical literature or national legend. The most famous choreographers of *dramballets* during these years were Rostislav Zakharov (*The Fountain of Bachchisarai,* 1934; and *Lost Illusions,* 1936) and Leonid Lavrovsky (*Prisoner of the Caucauses,* 1938; and *Romeo and Juliet,* 1940). Their productions were distinguished by clear-cut, efficient staging; a sequential series of actions; and developed personages that required dancing "in character" and acting. Above all, this meant dancing pantomime and dramatizing dance while rejecting big classical ensembles. Choreographers such as Vasily Vainonen (*The Flames of Paris*) and Vakhtang Chabukiani (*Heart of the Mountains, Laurencia*) aspired to great dance-ability. Indeed, the summer of 2009 witnessed the revival of excerpts from both *The Flames of Paris* and *Laurencia* on the Mariinsky stage with vibrant emotionality and bravura steps—floating *grands jetés,* airborne pyrotechnics, and wondrous strings of pirouettes.

The *dramballet* of the 1930s incorporated lyricism and psychological depth on the one hand (reaching its apogee in the art of Ulanova, Sergeyev, and Vecheslova) and expression and dynamism (Semënova and Dudinskaya) on the other hand, along with the development of virtuosity in male dancing, exemplified by such greats as Asaf Messerer and Vakhtang Chabukiani.[68]

The onset of *dramballet* trends, however, seemed to threaten the classical heritage. Just as she had demonstrated openness to Lopukhov's acrobatic steps, Vaganova also recognized the need for a new approach to ballet productions, one that incorporated the trends of socialist realism. Here again though, Vaganova did not believe that the classical heritage should be completely eliminated or ignored. In an address published in *Zhizn' Iskusstva* in 1925, she defended the necessity that the classics remain in coexistence with new styles of dance:

> The fact that you have Blok, Mayakovsky and others, does that mean that there should be no Pushkin, or that since Stravinsky and Prokofiev exist, Glinka, Borodin and Tchaikovsky's productions must disappear? If art must express modern life, then it doesn't mean that classical images and their past must disappear from the face of the earth.[69]

In a 1935 diary entry titled "New Ballet," she wrote:

> Between the conventionality of classical dance and the demands of "realism" there is no contradiction.... We only need to understand this [classical] dance as movement that is socially and emotionally sensible, bringing it into existence, building upon it the actions and movements of an artistic image. Thus it is approved through meaningful, realist-motivated, emotionally saturated dance. It is confirmed and created in our wonderful country, no where else in the world are such conditions for the growth and flourishing of genuine artistic talents created.[70]

With her 1935 assignment to revise *Esmeralda*, a ballet originally choreographed by Jules Perrot and subsequently revised by Petipa, Vaganova wrote that her task was to bring the production "as close as possible to the wonderful Hugo novel; to make the plot development as clear as possible, and the characters, passions, situations and general historical atmosphere as realistic as possible."[71] The ballet had been performed for seventy years at that point, and had undergone many changes during that period. Tsar Nikolas I had required the ending be changed to a happy one that, according to Vaganova, entailed the loss of the elements of social protest, as well as "brilliance, truthfulness, concrete characterization, and logic of dramatic action."[72]

She made the ballet more realistic without disrupting its classical style, which is noteworthy during a period of complete revisionist tendencies. In *Esmeralda*, Vaganova demonstrated the unlimited possibilities of classical form. She wrote, "The new requirements that we have of the ballet performance demand a sensible dramatic deployment of the subject, of character and concrete images, realistic veracity and passions."[73]

In revising *Esmeralda*, Vaganova sought to tidy up the "canon of choreography drama of the 19th century [using] a modern aesthetic."[74] Vaganova changed a few *mis-en-scènes* with the goal of giving greater emphasis to the social conflict. Her changes reflected the growing influence of social realism. She also adapted the *grand pas de deux* of *Diana and Acteon* in the last act, which depicted the myth of Diana, to help illustrate the general idea of the ballet. Using Diana's bow as a barrier between the couple, whose hands never touch, she choreographed a virtuoso duet that expressed the heroic character of the warlike Diana.[75] According to Lidia Evmentieva:

> In her productions, Vaganova tried to replace conventional ballet pantomime with particular gestures and expressive dancing action. She built dance on the difficult technique of the past, enriched by the findings of our modern classics. In *Esmeralda* she . . . demonstrated the unlimited possibilities of the classical form which changes with time in relation to its tasks, but always remains a source of the balletmaster's artistry.[76]

In contrast, Lopukhov chided Vaganova for her revisions to the ballet, stating:

> Vaganova's subsequent adaptation of this *pas* rendered it completely meaningless. Vaganova removed the part of the Satyr, thereby eliminating the conflict between Endymion and the Satyr that is the culmination of the whole ensemble; as a result, the work lost its narrative and choreographic harmony. I remember Petipa's Satyr well, as danced first by Georgy Kiasksht and later by Leonid Leontiev. The Satyr's leg jerked as if to kick away Endymion (originally Vaslav Nijinsky) who leapt over him in a *soubresaut*, while Diana (Anna Pavlova) took flight in *jetés*. Together the three enacted an unforgettable choreographic masterpiece. Alas, Petipa's

masterpiece was distorted by Vaganova, who failed to realize that the whole of Petipa's *pas de Diane* was brilliantly infused with the conflict between these characters.[77]

Historian Vera Krasovskaya noted that the choreography in the "Court of Miracles" scene was "weaker than its vivid costumes and makeup suggested. During rehearsals, Vaganova had continuously struggled with the dances of the multicolored crowd, but they remained monotonous, tediously symmetrical, and repetitive."[78] The twentieth-century audience became "bored watching the slow sequence of final episodes, beginning with a scene in the tavern."[79] However, loud applause, congratulations, and curtain calls crowned the close of the premiere on April 23, 1935, and the ballet was performed in Moscow later that year to critical acclaim. *Esmeralda* secured a place in the company's repertoire. Even today, although the full-length *Esmeralda* is no longer danced, the *Diana and Acteon pas de deux* is often performed at gala concerts and evenings of divertissements, yet another outlet for the technical virtuosity of the company's dancers, and a testament to Vaganova's legacy.

Of that successful Moscow tour in 1935, Konstantin Sergeyev noted, "People began to speak of ballet for the first time as if about a serious, deeply substantial art. And this was Vaganova's victory, her foresight, her belief in the orientation towards the task of Time, standing in front of Soviet art and, in part, in front of ballet."[80] Ballet was once again taken as seriously as it had been before the Revolution. After the *grand pas de deux* from *Diana and Acteon,* she moved on to the *The Fountain of Bachchisarai.*

It is said that the entire lexicon of other ballets also reflected Vaganova's influence. One example is *Laurencia* (1939), a ballet steeped with Mediterranean flair that portrays peasants defending themselves against a tyrant. It promised a new level of perfection and utilized the "heroic performer" that Vaganova had cultivated.[81] "To carefully preserve the great classical productions of world ballet art is one of the main tasks with a theatre such as ours, the Leningrad Theatre of Opera and Ballet," she wrote. "But, 'preserve' is hardly the same as ossification, static inertness, artistic death."[82]

A passionate advocate for the new trends in ballet, Vaganova wrote in her diary of the Soviet productions she thought worthy of preservation:

From the productions in the revolutionary years, the[se] new ballets in Leningrad and Moscow can be preserved in the repertoire: *The Red Poppy, Salambo, The Ice Maiden,* and the last talented successful one, *The Flames of Paris.* All the rest must be eliminated from the ballet repertoire as unsuccessful. [Though] *The Flames of Paris* was not made on a theme of today, it is understandable and clear as addressing the spirit of our time. The emancipation of the oppressed, that is, the class struggle, which led the French people into revolution, infects the viewer with its enthusiasm. The combination of the talented balletmaster and musician produced a true Soviet production. (1933)[83]

In another entry addressed to the task of choreographic education, she hinted at the achievements of Soviet ballet:

The new creative aspirations of the Soviet Theatre as a whole, and of Soviet choreography in part, led our school on a new path of academic methods . . . and called forth the necessary resolution of new problems which our pre-revolutionary ballet school did not and could not know."[84]

Her Contemporaries' Recollections

Numerous tributes, many from newspaper and magazine articles, record the impressions and memories of Vaganova by some of her most famous students. The following excerpts further illuminate her life and personality.

Natalia Dudinskaya, one of her prized pupils, attended Vaganova's "class of perfection," the daily lessons given only to those upper-level dancers who had achieved flawless technique and excellence in dancing. Dudinskaya discusses the close relationship she maintained with her teacher throughout her life:

When I studied in school, all the students passed through Vaganova's hands. She led the last three years of teaching. Of course Agrippina Yakovlevna had different students in her classes. Along with the very talented were average and sometimes weak ones, but all of them went out onstage from her class, and this allowed for a unified style, for which, in the course of several decades, our Leningrad Ballet became famous. This singular style ... appeared most brightly in the harmonious plastique and expressive arms, in the obedient flexibility and also the steel aplomb of the torso, in the noble and singular carriage of the head. All of Vaganova's students are characterized by this style, from artists [members] of the corps de ballet to leading ballerinas, and therein lies the distinguishing trait of Vaganova's school.

I trusted Vaganova immediately, from the first moment, deferring to her passionately all of my life. She became my singular pedagogue in the course of my artistic profession, my friend, my counselor, my second mother. She defined my path in art, my view of it, my taste, my views. In difficult moments of my life she supported me morally with all of her soul, with all of her warm and sincere heart; together with me she experienced all of my successes and joys.

I studied with Vaganova for 23 years—three years in school and twenty in the class of perfection that she held in the theatre for ballet artists. . . . It seems to me I never worked with such attention, effort, and self-sacrifice as I did in the first year with Vaganova.

Agrippina Yakovlevna spoke very softly, teaching us to pay strict attention. She explained simply and understandably. She showed the combinations only twice, once on each leg. But how wonderful those demonstrations were. During the lesson she didn't sit in one place, but walked around the classroom, looking at our execution from various angles. Nothing escaped her, she saw everything, noticed the tiniest sins. Agrippina Yakovlevna was very strict, demanding, and uncompromising. She watched each of us vigilantly. She had a special approach to each student. For her, teaching didn't stop at the bell. With her dear, all-seeing eyes she followed all of our lives. Coming to her in the 7th year of school (there were 9 years of schooling then), it was as if we were once again first year students. Beginning with "A," the position of the torso and arms.[85]

Ballerina Alla Shelest recalled Vaganova's legacy and lessons:

For 29 years the pedagogical artistry of Vaganova has been accepted by many generations of artists. They all surmise what she gave the school: freedom without unnecessary strain of the musculature and ligaments that surmounts any technical difficulty of dance, [and the ability to] reproduce the style of any ballet performance. And it must be said that Agrippina Yakovlevna looked at a lesson as comprehensive, developed mastery, [involving both] artistry and endurance, and never considered the daily hour of class just a warm-up for the days' rehearsals. For her everything served a main purpose: to create a deep and poetic image in the best performance, which was always just ahead.[86]

... The [Vaganova] method consists of the mastery of the most difficult technical coordinations in which not a single position, even at first glance the most meaningless one, is lost, and the invisibility of the technique itself. Mastery of her method gave the artist the possibility of full freedom in plastique to express the choreographic text, and created a premise for the absolute clarity of its statement.

[At] the foundation [of Vaganova's] teaching . . . lies harmony, purity of classical form and the physical laws of motion. They help [the dancer] to overcome any difficulty in technique, to reproduce any choreographic style, to give meaning to dance, and to extend the stage life of the actress. In her lessons, Vaganova demanded the fulfillment of dancing phrases from her students, and the ability to single out the main movement in relief. The connecting movements for her held a supporting role, and in practice I myself subsequently managed to achieve the correctness she demanded. . . . Working in class, Agrippina Yakovlevna trained us to analytical thinking.[87]

Historian Galina Kremshevskaya, in an article about Vaganova's life and work, discussed Agrippina Yakovlevna's entry to the art of pedagogy:

Fame came to Vaganova in the post-revolutionary years and was connected to her teaching. Fulfilling her activities on the stage of the Mariinsky Theatre did not bring her particular joy, but she became a . . . master of pedagogy. Also a student of the Petersburg ballet school, an artist and later leading ballerina, Vaganova had a feeling of dissatisfaction. She understood that great Russian ballet and its traditions exist with bright talent, and gifted performances.

But (perhaps most importantly) there was no single unified school, no single method of teaching. There was no scientific approach to teaching dance skill. The decision to engage in pedagogy was immediately made as she left the stage. All of her school and artistic path were preparation for this.

N[ikolai] P. Ivanovsky, artistic director of the school, observed Vaganova's work for many years and thought that she, "led the knowledge of Soviet dance pedagogy to the height of teaching at the highest academic levels. Even the best pre-revolutionary pedagogues could not dream of this. Vaganova never stopped in her searches. As a true artist she always had the expectation and interest to look towards her creative tomorrows."

Recounting Vaganova's special methods, Dudinskaya rushes to open its path to those who are not familiar with the secrets of the ballet trade: "You don't have to be a particular connoisseur in the field of ballet to observe in our theatre's performances that everyone, from the *corps de ballet* to the leading ballerinas, has a general manner of execution. A single style, a united point of dance, appearing brighter than ever in the harmonious *plastique* of movement and the expressiveness of the arms, in the responsive suppleness and at the same time the iron aplomb of the torso, the noble and natural placement of the head—these are the distinguishing characteristics of Vaganova's school. The grammar of Vaganova helps to achieve full freedom of dance. We know that dance when we master it fully, brings huge joy. The struggle for this freedom is difficult and even torturous. Agrippina Yakovlevna devoted her life so that the struggle will not be in vain, so as to uncover the laws of mastery of the heights of dance; and not to give into the will of circumstance."[88]

Kremshevskaya noted also that Vaganova was equally unforgiving of herself as she was of her students, stating that Agrippina was

a demanding and strict counselor. Ruthless towards herself, she was ruthless towards others. Her verdict was always final. Praise was always deserved, never overstated. Vaganova had no patience for laziness, for distraction, for lack of discipline. The coincidental success of dancers who were not working systematically had no value to her. With special attention she worked with students, even those who were not particularly talented, but who shared her obsession for work. With such students she now and then created genuine miracles. When the working capacity of a ballerina came along with talent, for Vaganova that was an artistic celebration. ... The celebration for Vaganova was the graduation of her brilliant students. All of them were raised in her intelligent and exacting school. And all were completely different.[89]

Marina Semënova is said to have been not only one of Vaganova's prize pupils, but also her favorite. To form a portrait of these direct descendents of Vaganova's careful coaching, we can read what those who saw them dance thought at the time. The dancer Mikhail Mikhailov, in his book *Early Years of the Leningrad Ballet,* noted the heights of Vaganova's life achievements and concluded: "If Vaganova taught only Semënova how to dance, it would have been enough of a remnant of herself to leave behind the fame of the best pedagogue of her time."[90] That Agrippina Yakovlevna did so much more than that speaks to the revolutionary Renaissance woman that she was. Semënova herself retained fond memories of her pedagogue:

> Everything connected to her name was for me always the joy of life, joy of my existence on stage, joy of love and belief in it and in my teacher. She freed me from a technical path, gave me color ... revived the torso, arms, [and] body, gave new, deep meaning to all the dancing poses. Vaganova gave full freedom to the artistic blooming of the artist.
> She was convinced that through strictness and accuracy each dance combination, each composition of academic movement must lead to artistry.
> ... She always demanded, "even better, reveal something new." It is interesting that she never "wore us out completely" in rehearsals, but in lessons she "wrung us out" fully.[91]

If they were performing that evening, the dancers were allowed to hold energy in reserve; otherwise they were expected to exhaust their energies in class in the pursuit of perfection. Marina Semënova's dancing has been characterized by many as one of the best of her era. Film clips of

Semënova reveal a stout dancer with strong legs who appears to have nothing in common with today's ballerinas in either physique or technique. But at the time she was lauded for her perfection of form. Kremshevskaya explained the traits that made this unlikely star so captivating:

Simplicity, a powerful belief in dance, and perfect form—all [of] which characterize the features of Vaganova's method—all of this was contained in Semënova's dance. The expansive movements of the young dancer, her unusually beautiful arms, at times singing a special sort of Russian harmony, her dance knew no chance, checked and exact, its revolution ending in strong-willed poses of mysterious beauty. . . . Semënova forever remains a great legend in ballet. Even if in former graduations there were talented dancers, she will eternally be listed as the first student of Vaganova's famous school. For good reason Semënova succeeded in succinctly formulating the basic thesis of her pedagogue's method: "She demanded that in the dance there be an image, emotion, substance transmitted by the whole body. After all, the body is our instrument. And it is because she took care [and devoted herself], that this instrument can be developed to perfection.[92]

In his article on Vaganova, Nikolai Anisimov, a student of hers who became a Kirov Ballet character dancer, illuminated the stern energy and passion that infused her work:

She was always so internally collected, so energetic, so fault-finding, strict and at the same time followed each of our movements with such passion that even the most usual movement of a class exercise, one well-known by heart, in her presence acquired new, special interest. Not one student could escape her intent gaze.

She understood perfectly that the language of musical movement which we speak in our modern ballet theatre is conventional, a "classical" language. And she demanded that the dancers speak it easily, fluently, using all of its rich possibilities. Mastering it perfectly, they were unrestricted to express in it what was attractive to them.[93]

A few of Vaganova's students are still alive. Aside from Irina Trofimova, who spoke earlier of Vaganova's influence on the *port de bras* in

Swan Lake, there is Alla Osipenko, now a coach at the Mikhailovsky The-atre in Petersburg. A reed-thin woman with short blonde hair and the physique of a young ballerina, Osipenko has a calm, open manner that is almost an anomale in today's world of Russian ballet. Often described as a black sheep whose early career was overshadowed by the drama caused by Nureyev and Makarova's defections, Osipenko nonetheless enjoyed a distinctive career that included collaboration with innovative choreogra-phers such as Boris Eifman and Leonid Yakobson. Speaking at length to me in her dressing room at the Mikhailovsky after a long day of rehears-als,[94] she smiled fondly as memories of Vaganova return to her:

> As a person she was very interesting. Her authority was unques-tionable, and everyone feared her, including me. She could offend you or hit you on the leg. But you would never see any tenderness from her, that was completely impossible. She was much more de-manding towards me because I was very lazy.

A lifted eyebrow prompted Osipenko to support her claim.

> Oh, I had good physical attributes, but my laziness outshone my positive traits. She was very demanding of me, and very often she would glare at me for something I didn't do right.
>
> One day when we were in Moscow, I was still a student at the Choreographic Institute [Vaganova Academy], at the time danc-ing *The Nutcracker*. She said something to me in rehearsal that had offended me so much that I cried all day long. And as I sat that evening in the dressing room, putting on makeup for the evening performance, suddenly the door opened and I felt a tangerine fall into my lap. I looked up. Agrippina Yakovlevna had thrown the fruit to me and had already disappeared. But I understood with the tangerine that inside her there was something different from what she projected outside to others. She was that sort of person, it wasn't that you don't do something correctly, it's that you cannot do what she is asking. She didn't become more tender from that episode, but even more demanding.

Vaganova's harshness with her pupils was part of her character. Osip-enko explained that during her first year of work in the company, again

Alla Osipenko as the Mistress of the Copper Mountain in *The Stone Flower*, a ballet by Yuri Grigorovich that brought Osipenko considerable notoriety in Russia for her unique physicality and plastique. Photo: Mariinsky Theatre Archives.

Above: Alla Osipenko as the Lilac Fairy in *The Sleeping Beauty*. Her talents in adagio and long lines found expression in this role, one she danced before leaving the Kirov Theatre. Photo: Mariinsky Theatre Archives.

Right: Alla Osipenko as Odette in *Swan Lake*. Osipenko has said that ballets in which she could not relate to the character held little interest for her. Photo: Mariinsky Theatre Archives.

preparing for a performance of *The Nutcracker*, Vaganova had already fallen ill. But even her poor health did not prevent her from continuing to work.

She invited me to her home and we rehearsed as she lay in her bed. And she was just as demanding and just as harsh as ever! One day after such a rehearsal, as I was leaving she said to me, "There's a box there, take a piece of candy."

I said, "Thank you Agrippina Yakovlevna, but I don't want one."

She said, "Take a candy."

I said, "Thank you Agrippina Yakovlevna, but I don't want one."

Then she shouted, "What did I tell you to do?! Take a candy!"

Osipenko emitted a relaxed laugh at the memory of Vaganova's sternness. "She was a very emotional person! They called her the 'Queen of Variations' and she received the title ballerina only one year to her retirement." More seriously, Osipenko explained, "It was hard. Her profession, while she was dancing, did not come easily to her. And so she very much wanted to see in her students what she didn't achieve in her own life."

Indeed, when Vaganova's former students, Dudinskaya and Shelest, were already ballerinas, Osipenko and Kolpakova, Vaganova's last pupils, were twenty years younger and just beginning their careers. Tiuntina, a teacher at the School, asked Vaganova what she thought of these two young dancers. With utter modesty, Osipenko spoke frankly about the episode: "Vaganova said an interesting thing: 'About Kolpakova I am not at all worried, she will be a good classical dancer. But Osipenko for me is abstract.'" Vaganova saw Kolpakova as a clear-cut case for success, but Osipenko's personality was something that Vaganova could not quite grasp. Osipenko elaborated:

She evidently didn't understand my laziness, because I had been lazy when I was born and Agrippina Yakovlevna worried about it, tried to understand what to do with me.

You know how they say, "protection," now, referring to those who look after you. My godmother, my two grandmothers raised me, I had no father, and my mother worked. My godmother was a dressmaker in Leningrad. And when Agrippina Yakovlevna was no longer with us, my godmother told me, "You know Lalya-sha (as they called me then), I clothed Agrippina Yakovlevna, I was her dressmaker."

Agrippina Yakovlevna never allowed me to understand that she was somehow connected to me. My godmother never told me either. Agrippina Yakovlevna was always stricter with me than with her other students, so it could never have entered my head. Only once I had noticed Agrippina Yakovlevna's blouse and thought to myself in passing, "how interesting, that blouse looks like the ones my godmother sews," but it never occurred to me!

Osipenko finished this story with laughter too, recalling the duplicate blouses. "At that time there were no ready-made clothes in stores; it was all dressmakers. But she never led anyone to discover that she was connected to my family in some way. So this is also a surprising quality of hers." Osipenko shook her head, "Startling."

Irina Trofimova still holds clear memories of the training she received from Agrippina Yakovlevna. Trofimova recalled her pedagogue's manner:

Agrippina Yakovlevna of course was not just a talented pedagogue. Her personal qualities included boldness, wisdom, directness—she never feared speaking the truth—and criticism, which always helps others in the desire to understand things. She told us a lot about herself and about ballet, how she tried to understand the method of the Italians, how we first had French teachers, and then Cecchetti, and Legnani, the prima ballerina, came. She tried to understand why they turned so well. She unified the best of the French and Italian schools.

Vaganova's qualities also included stubbornness, will and strong character, both in dancing and in teaching. As teaching qualities, she had musicality. As a pedagogue the coordination of movement in dance is very important, not just the eyes and the head.

For the Pedagogical Faculty, we studied in the studio with Vaganova, with a piano and a barre. She lectured us, had us do the steps, and corrected us. Separately, Kostrovitskaya led training classes at 8:30 in the morning where we strengthened our knowledge. For all of the special classes we went to the School, but for history of the theatre and academic courses we went to the Conservatory.

Later Vaganova invited us to her own lessons with students. She taught us to notice the students' mistakes—because there are pedagogues who know the method but cannot see the flaws in execution. Of course this is a quality gained from experience. Why is that girl not standing on her leg? Why is she falling back?

Trofimova gave a present-day example of the difference between the properly trained pedagogues and other coaches.

I sit on the exam council now and a certain teacher was sitting next to me. "Do you see how her foot isn't leaving the floor properly?" I remarked of one student. That teacher couldn't say anything. She knows the general rules, but she doesn't see the connection between the rules and the mistakes.

In each class [year/level] we have certain steps that the students must master. Every pedagogue has certain steps to teach that year in a defined rhythm, and that is Vaganova's method—the execution of the steps so they are clean and correct.

Her method was a basic, scientific approach to lessons that helps you to master the body in perfect form and technique. The classics help you to dance other styles too. We're stronger in our method because it doesn't only provide naked technique, it also opens the soul to the content of the dance.

Methodology Department

In 1934, Vaganova published her book, *Osnovy Klassicheskogo Tantsa* (published in English as *Basic Principles of Classical Ballet*). This coincided with the adoption of her method by the Leningrad Choreographic Institute as the main system for training dancers. In many ways an academic manual for teachers of classical dance, the textbook was used not only in Russia; it was republished numerous times and translated into many foreign languages. With its appearance in other countries, letters flooded into Vaganova's mailbox from readers in Holland, Germany, and elsewhere thanking her for her contribution, and lamenting the lack of teachers like her in their own countries.

On Vaganova's suggestion, a Pedagogical Faculty was opened inside the School that same year, as well as a national department to teach citizens from the various Soviet republics in the Vaganova system. Through this department, Vaganova's method of teaching spread throughout Russia.

Two years later, the textbook served as a resource for courses on pedagogy given at the Leningrad Choreographic School. Pedagogues Lidia Tiuntina, Elena Shiripina, Nadezhda Bazarova, Varvara Mei, and others took the course and went on to teach at the Choreographic School.

Vaganova herself had to approve the teachers who taught at the School. Led by experience and intuition, she chose Tiuntina, then age thirty-five, who "listened and asked pointed questions," and Vera Kostrovitskaya, who had taught Vaganova's own teacher, Olga Preobrajenska. In Kostrovitskaya, Vaganova found a like-minded critical thinker and assistant. The two discussed the details of technique, and Kostrovitskaya went on to write her own book of ballet lessons. Others, such as Varvara Mei and Nadezhda Bazarova, also joined the pedagogical faculty under Vaganova.

In the 1930s, the uniquely Soviet, almost clinical approach to ballet helped push the art forward. In addition to socialist realism, Vaganova's efforts, and codification of the training system, the new pedagogy was supported by a Methodology Department at the Choreographic Institute in which male and female specialists worked on teaching the method. Dancer and teacher Konstantin Shatilov recalled the specialists of this department in an interview before his death in 2003:

> They visited all the classes and paid attention to mistakes. Under Konstantin Mikhailovich Sergeyev, the teachers came and consulted these specialists in methodology who could send in a knowledgeable teacher for consultation. Now, the Methodology Department is closed, and our pedagogues each learn on their own. We need to reinstate the Methodology Department. It is very bad that our examinations take place without any discussion. You have to have a discussion, a methodology conference in order to

help the pedagogues correct errors. We are afraid that this will lead to bad relations, or offense will be taken. [But] insofar as there is no serious control and demand, then each person will carry their "own" [version], and slowly Vaganova's method will collapse.[95] [See Chapter 3 for Asylmuratova's defense of the current system of methodology.]

During Agrippina Yakovlevna's lifetime, the teachers in the school were educated by Vaganova herself, or later at the Faculty of Pedagogy in the Leningrad State Conservatory.[96]

From the comments of those who knew her, we receive a picture of the famous pedagogue as a woman of high energy whose career was all-consuming. "Developing the science of dance, Vaganova never became a supporter of dry methodology. At the debut of her graduating students, she displayed the artistic values of her quest, their end goal. Her vigilant eye never missed any artistic individuality or distinctive gifts," wrote Kremshevskaya.[97]

Vaganova received the title of Professor of Choreography on June 19, 1943, and on August 16 of that year was named a People's Artist of the RSFSR (Russian Soviet Federal Socialist Republic), when she was simultaneously given the job of Consultant to the Bolshoi Theatre while maintaining her work as a professor in the Leningrad Choreographic School.

Vaganova, it is said, was "everywhere at once." A workaholic, she toiled endlessly, assuming responsibilities that others could have fulfilled but which she trusted only to herself.[98] Blok describes in detail where Agrippina Yakovlevna could be found in the course of a typical day: in the costume department, in the infirmary (tending to sick students), observing the teachers of the younger classes, in the administrative offices, managing the number of ballet performances per week, or discussing the authors of a new libretto. And of course in daily classes and rehearsals, and nightly in the director's box, watching performances. Even on her deathbed, she worried about her last student, Irina Kolpakova, and how her preparations for performances were faring. Kolpakova remembers that the ailing Agrippina Yakovlevna was "interested in how they would prepare my small first roles. After her death, her son's wife told me that in her last days Agrippina Yakovlevna remembered me as one of her last students whose fate concerned her."[99]

Vaganova devoted her life to her students and her work and made massive strides in the name of Soviet and Russian ballet pedagogy in the span of her lifetime.

3

~

CVaganova Today

Her Students

For those who knew her, Vaganova held an important place in their lives. Nearly sixty years after her death, Vaganova's traditions are still continued by her pupils. The discussions with eight pedagogues that follow illuminate their opinions on the current state of training at the Vaganova Academy, to what extent they believe the Vaganova style and tradition is being preserved by the Mariinsky Theatre, and the development of ballet technique in general.

The Role of Pedagogue

Unique to the Vaganova-Mariinsky organization is the rigorous and insular pedagogy designed to preserve tradition and shield the style, for the most part, from outside influence. In Russia, pedagogues are much more than simple "coaches" in the Western sense of the term. A pedagogue is a former dancer who has gone through the full nine years of training at the Vaganova Academy, received a diploma, danced in a professional Russian theater, and then completed the Vaganova Academy's graduate program for pedagogues, which is approximately four years in length. Only after passing that set of examinations can the dancer be called a "pedagogue" and be allowed to coach other dancers in the theater or teach in the school.

In the pedagogical system, dancers who studied under Vaganova herself or, more recently, those who have passed through the school system, often perform on stage and, once retired, begin to coach the younger generation. Others may not perform as much, but they still receive the required teaching diploma in order to teach in the School. Thus the Vaganova methods are preserved orally, through words, and physically, through demonstration of specific movements and body positions or, as the Russians prefer to say, the traditions are passed along "from hand to hand, from foot to foot." Teachers and coaches trained in other ballet schools are banned—unless a Westerner arrives to set a new addition to the ballet's repertoire, which is then a case of staging within the theater and not one of training the dancers in their own heritage—and the details of the classical Vaganova-Mariinsky style are singular, never mixed. Those who train future generations have all received the same education at the Vaganova Academy.

Additionally, in the Mariinsky there is a correct way of performing each classical role and, for that matter, each classical step. Variation and individuality in terms of technique—the placement of arms or head, the execution of batterie, or the way a *jeté* is approached—are not allowed; the dancers are trained in the same system, and this is visible especially when observing the Mariinsky corps de ballet. Attention to detail is paramount. In each role, in each step or pose or movement, the inclination of the head, the angle of a wrist or elbow can make a huge difference, not only in the effect on the viewer but on whether the dancer is executing the movement properly. "Properly," in this lexicon, means according to tradition, according to Vaganova's style, and also "the way it has always been done." In the Vaganova technique, there is a correct way, and usually only one correct way, to perform a step.

In addition to technique, however, dramatic expression must also be cultivated. Discussing this crucial component of dance, Vaganova herself wrote the following:

> Why does classical dance so move the viewer? Because the task of the dances [performed] with such lightness, without emphasizing effort, achieved by painstaking work, is a victory. Of course it is not

the definitive victory of an artist. Expression, meaningfulness, that is what we aim for.[1]

What was this great pedagogue herself like? Galina Petrovna Kekisheva is one of Vaganova's last remaining students. She graduated in 1948 and danced with the Kirov until 1971, performing solo roles such as Amour in *Don Quixote*, the *pas de deux* from *The Flames of Paris*, and the Nocturne in *Chopiniana*. She conducted the Kirov's class of perfection after 1971 and continues to work at the Mariinsky. A petite woman, Kekisheva carries herself with a grace that speaks of another era entirely. Although a dancer of the Soviet era with sharp opinions to match, Kekisheva's shock of white hair and smart eyeglasses lend her the appearance of a warm grandmother, a mother hen looking after her chicks. At the Mariinsky, she does just that, continuing to uphold the strict Vaganova traditions in her classes and rehearsals. Kekisheva coaches many notable dancers, including Valeria Martiniouk and Evgenia Obratsova. She also teaches two women's classes each morning. She agreed to discuss Vaganova's pedagogy in one of the theater's dressing rooms, a small space with old couches and several makeup mirrors shared by some of the Mariinsky's leading coaches.[2] As we sat down, she was forthright and open in her recollections of Vaganova.

"Vaganova had a very strong character," Kekisheva begins. "She could get people to believe in her, and get them to do things. She would correct the pedagogues, the manner in which they would teach a certain step, ensuring the unified method at the Leningrad Choreographic Institute. She went around the classes of the pedagogues and corrected each pedagogue, how they taught the method, where the leg is in *coup de pied*, how the leg goes back into *arabesque*."

"Vaganova saw the individuals who had a talent for teaching," Kekisheva continues. "After all, not every ballerina who has danced many performances can be a pedagogue, moreover a rehearsal coach. Vaganova very clearly and very carefully looked after the school and her system. She watched, and would take into the Pedagogy Department people she saw and realized, 'Yes, this person can be a pedagogue.' This tradition supported the style of the theater, the style of the company."

Konstantin Shatilov, a former teacher at the Vaganova Academy, made a similar point in his recollections of Agrippina Yakovlevna:

Galina Kekisheva in the role of Pasquale, early in her career. Kekisheva is one of Vaganova's last students and continues to coach leading ballerinas of the Mariinsky Theatre today. Photo courtesy of the Mariinsky Theatre archives.

A pedagogue must know psychology, the workload of the students in the theater. There must be an individual approach to each student. But above all he must master the Vaganova method. Then the pedagogue will be a good specialist. Not every ballet dancer can be a teacher. You need a special talent for this profession. It is important so that the student correctly absorbs each element—the form, manner, and cleanliness of execution depend on this. But first it is necessary to unfold it, to achieve mastery. To execute difficult technical things with ease. Ballet also has simple movements which are difficult to do. Even walking or running around the stage, you must be able to do. I often see many dancers run onstage with bent knees.[3]

Finding, selecting, and training pedagogues continues today at the Vaganova Academy. (See the interview with Asylmuratova later in the chapter for more information on this topic.) But as Shatilov and Kekisheva imply, the pedagogue does not simply regurgitate steps and classical choreography. Ludmila Adeyeva, the author of several books on ballet pedagogy, writes that the tasks of the pedagogue include

forming the artistic personality of the student, cultivating their artistic tastes, musicality, developing their work ethic, a strong will, love, and devotion to the art of dance. Along with it, the pedagogue-trainer is a sculptor, working daily to create living beauty on the human body, the body of a graceful, strong, dutiful, responsive instrument of expression of the human soul's feelings through plastique.

The description is a broad one. It goes without saying that the role of teacher in classical dance is important in the development of a ballet artist, no matter what country he or she hails from. In Russia especially, pedagogues have a much greater role in the artists' formation and throughout their career than they do in most other countries. Adeyeva notes that the pedagogue must also be a "psychologist, to prepare the pupil for independent work in adult life."[4]

Retired Kirov ballerina Gabriela Komleva, an Honored Artist and a People's Artist of the USSR (1983), and the laureate of numerous ballet competitions including the International Ballet Competition at Varna in 1966, is a well-known, outspoken supporter of the old style who frequently contributes candid, opinionated articles to the Vaganova Academy's publication *Vestnik*. Komleva studied under Vera Kostrovitskaya, Vaganova's head assistant and the author of a book on ballet technique that is, because of the two women's close collaboration, almost as important a reference manual as the one by Vaganova herself. An active woman in every sense, years ago Komleva instituted a higher education course at the Rimsky-Korsakov Conservatory across the street from the Mariinsky Theatre. Her program continues to train balletmaster-*répétiteurs*, which is, as she explains, a designation slightly more prestigious than simple *répétiteur* (rehearsal coach), a title that can be conferred by the Vaganova Academy. Komleva writes the syllabus herself and continues to oversee the course. However, despite her firm views on all theater-related issues, Komleva's welcoming smile and soft eyes portray the image of a warm, surprisingly open woman. She willingly shared her views on the state of the Mariinsky today.[5]

According to Komleva, the role of the pedagogue in Russian ballet has hardly changed.

> It is a very important part of the life of any ballerina, and moreover, it's not just temporary. The ballerina needs a pedagogue throughout her career; the entire time there must be a pair of eyes that sees and critiques things. Things must be controlled from the side, and only then can there be progress. Very often your internal sensations do not coincide with external appearance, and the ballerina may think everything is fine, but the pedagogue must see what the ballerina is attempting to achieve with a certain role or step.

Tatiana Terekhova, a Soviet-era ballerina, studied with Ninella Kurgapkina and Irina Kolpakova, and as such is already a third-generation recipient of Vaganova training. She graduated in 1970, and, after twenty-eight years performing roles that included Odette-Odile, Myrtha, Kitri, and Aurora, she worked with the Boston Ballet as a rehearsal coach from 1998 to 2000. Terekhova today coaches dancers at the Mariinsky Theatre, among them the controversial principal dancer Alina Somova, and recent graduate Anastasia Nikitina, both wispy women with 190-degree extensions. Easily recognizable by her tidily cropped blonde hair and slender frame, Terekhova is known for her seriousness in rehearsals.

Gabriela Komleva today. She still coaches inside the Mariinsky and heads a course for pedagogues at the Rimsky-Korsakov Conservatory. Photo: Oleg Zotov.

Gabriela Komleva as the Firebird. Photo: Mariinsky Theatre Archives.

Gabriela Komleva as Raymonda. Komleva was a leading name in the theater during the Soviet years. Photo: Mariinsky Theatre Archives.

Tatiana Terekhova as Kitri from *Don Quixote* (1978). Terekhova's bravado technique is visible here. Photo: Yulia Larionova.

Right: Terekhova as
Kitri in 1987. Photo:
Yulia Larionova.

Below: Ninella
Kurgapkina coaching
Tatiana Terekhova
inside studio 5 at the
Mariinsky Theatre
in 1982. Photo: Yulia
Larionova.

Everything about her, her thoughts, her speech, and her approach to her art, seems an essay in efficiency.[6] Terekhova contributes her thoughts on the pedagogue's role, stating frankly, "You give your mind, your attention, and your efforts to your pedagogue. If you have a real, genuine pedagogue, he or she directs you your entire life. And thank God, not one day in my career was I without a pedagogue, I always had an eye there looking after me. I consider the pedagogue to be the foundation; they play a main role in the ballerina's career."

But presence and psychological understanding alone are not enough. A pedagogue must have certain traits in order to cultivate a ballerina and help her achieve success.

Former Kirov ballerina Ninella Alexandrovna Kurgapkina has coached some of the Mariinsky Ballet's leading ballerinas, including Zhanna Ayupova, Uliana Lopatkina, and soloist Tatiana Tkachenko. Judging purely by her size, one would never assume the diminutive pedagogue to be such a loud, outspoken, and forthright woman. Utterly Soviet in style—she was known to wear peasant-style head scarves to receptions at St. Petersburg's elegant Hotel Astoria, and she refused to have her hair done for her jubilee celebration in February 2009—during our interviews Kurgapkina was edged with a roughness that only years of Communist living can create. Indeed, she was one of the few ballerinas who danced with Rudolf Nureyev before he left Russia, her own dancing career spanning over thirty years, from 1947 to 1981. Known for her bravura style, she excelled as Kitri, but danced a wide range of roles, from Odette-Odile, Aurora, and Giselle, to some of Leonid Yacobson's "Choreographic Miniatures." Kurgapkina taught the class of perfection at the Kirov beginning in 1969, and from 1982 to 1990 was a pedagogue at the Leningrad Choreographic Institute (Vaganova Academy). Lovable, open, but firm in her views, Ninella Alexandrovna speaks adamantly about all of the topics discussed on the pages that follow.[7]

"First of all you have to have patience for the students," Ninella Kurgapkina explains, "so that they understand. And you have to demonstrate the combinations and the steps extremely clearly. Agrippina Yakovlevna said the most important responsibility of a pedagogue is to demonstrate well. How you show something, especially to small children, that is how they are going to do it from then on. And that is exactly true. Because if the child hasn't learned the coordination, catching up later is not

A rehearsal inside the Mariinsky Theatre. Ninella Kurgapkina, former partner of Rudolf Nureyev before his defection to the West, coaches him with Zhanna Ayupova in *La Sylphide*. The performance was Nureyev's last on the Mariinsky stage. Photo: Mariinsky Theatre Archives.

possible. It's the same in the army, when they don't take boys into the army who walk with the right arm and the right leg moving forward at the same time. That is the most frightening thing, the absence of coordination. And it is precisely the presence of coordination that sets the students of Vaganova apart, because all of those poses, when you transfer from one pose to another, it is like a motif, like a song. It creates the best impression when you look at a person and you want to repeat the image they've created. That is Vaganova."

Ninella Kurgapkina in 1957 as Kitri, one of her signature roles. Kurgapkina was known as a spitfire on stage. Photo: Efraim Lesov.

The Jubilee performance onstage the Mariinsky Theatre in spring 2009, in honor of Ninella Kurgapkina. She passed away just months after this photograph was taken. Photo: Natalia Razina.

Vaganova herself recorded the following thoughts on this topic:

Frequently the ballet artist who can no longer perform on stage or who has simply lost the ability to work hard turns to pedagogy. Do they really think it is so simple? They're mistaken. Many are students, but not everyone learns."[8]

That teaching is a thankless, difficult profession seems clear from such comments. As recently as 2004, however, Konstantin Shatilov bemoaned the shift toward a more lax selection process when it came to what certain pedagogues were teaching:

Previously the pedagogues were selected very seriously. When I was a student, classical dance was taught by the principal dancers—Boris Vasilievich Shavrov, Nikolai Alexeyevich Zubkovsky, [Alexander Ivanovich] Pushkin, [Alexei Afanasievich] Pisarev. They could correctly demonstrate how to execute difficult movements, but also simple ones. We were taught by pedagogues who knew their profession. There is the point of view that in order to teach you do not have to be able to do it yourself. I hold a different opinion, and believe that a pedagogue cannot show a student a movement that he hasn't done himself. Classical dance has its secrets, you cannot explain them, but you can give them, practically speaking, to someone else. They aren't written in any book. Vaganova never taught what she had not done herself. For example, in rehearsals for Strauss' *Waltz* that I danced with Ninella Kurgapkina, Vaganova advised me to consult a [male] pedagogue who taught *pas de deux*. Now as a rule in rehearsals, *pas de deux* is willingly taught by female pedagogues. It seems to me that each must work only in his own area.[9]

Although older pedagogues vary in their opinions, in her book, former ballerina Tatiana Vecheslova elucidated Shatilov's point further, explaining how the first generation of Soviet ballet pedagogues made a significant mark on the world not only by the famous dancers they produced but also in their manner of work:

The pedagogues who surrounded and raised us were our caretakers, spiritual counselors, instilling in us a love of art, respect for people, honest unselfishness, and a sense of camaraderie. But there was no discussion of material interests. No thoughts of career or of encouraging travel abroad, which often stimulates actors, none of that. There was one aspiration, one goal: to give yourself to art.

For Vecheslova, the role of pedagogue is a broad but important one.

Maybe the dancer can jump well, but not be harmonious in *tours* [*en l'air*], maybe he turns well but doesn't know the laws of behavior on stage, can't relate to his partner, doesn't understand how to enter the ballet, doesn't listen to the music, poorly allocates his physical strength, remembers the order of steps with difficulty, and so on.

But time is limited. Sometimes for studying and preparing a main role there is one month (that is good!), sometimes in extreme situations, ten or five days, or even only two days. The coach is still obliged to launch the dancer into the performance.

... [The pedagogue]'s first task is to preserve the individuality of the dancers. ... Just as important ... is reflection, pause, analysis, and with it the intensive mind-work, the mobilization of nerves, muscles, and temperament.[10]

So the pedagogue-*répétiteur* of ballet is not just a trainer and not simply a teacher. This profession to me is wider, more complex, more limited. The *répétiteur* must be a psychologist and pedagogue in the highest meaning of the word. It is difficult to achieve, but must be attempted. Launching the dancer into the court of specta-tors . . . After all, the ballet artist, even a young one, is not a school child. He can have (and should have!) his point of view on art, on new roles he plays, and the job of the pedagogue-*répétiteur* is not to dictate, but to help him find the path of truth.[11]

Having established the complex responsibilities inherent in the role of pedagogue, one can observe how pedagogues today are continuing the work of their predecessors—or at least trying to. Gabriela Komleva admits that she believes the manner of teaching the Vaganova style has already shifted: "After all, her textbook is called *Osnovye* or *The 'Foun-dation' of Classical Dance*, [also translated as "basic principles"] which means the basis of the classics. She always said that you should develop and perfect it, that you can leave it as is, but you can to add to it. Her students and the teachers who she trained, they did this, they worked on perfecting it, they didn't change anything of the old, but they added something, they sought a method of teaching, a method of *how* to carry out the teaching. And that is what made the school famous. What they taught me, is taught differently now, I think. Of course, the basic meth-ods are kept, but it is changing."

Preserving Tradition

What of this oral tradition, this rich legacy of Vaganova? Recent discus-sions among ballet historians, balletomanes, and even those inside the Mariinsky Theatre center around this very theme: is the style changing, or being preserved? Has time altered the Vaganova traditions, or is what we see on stage at the Mariinsky Theatre still representative of the Va-ganova method of technique as it should be danced?

The views, as one would guess, are mixed. The Mariinsky Ballet re-mains one of a kind worldwide, but within the theater, the nuances of what was done in the past and how dancers perform today is a very delicate subject.

Although she studied under Agrippina Vaganova for six years, Alla Osipenko nonetheless claims it is difficult to characterize Vaganova's method:

> I have my own opinion about if you can discuss her method or system. She was a genius pedagogue. Simply genius. In 1934 she wrote her book *Basic Principles of Classical Dance*. When I studied under her, it was the end of the '40s, beginning of the '50s, and she had changed many things written in that book. So when they say now, "I teach Vaganova's system" or "I base my lessons on Vaganova's method," my approach is that we don't know her system. She is too brilliant that we, simply her students, middle-level pedagogues, could repeat her. Every day she did something new, searched for something . . . and her method was *her personal* method, her personal system.

Osipenko explains the place of Vaganova as somewhat outside the circle of pedagogues who now support and transfer her training to others. Humbly, she adds, "I consider that we, her students, can pass on only the style of her teaching. Our task is not to *spoil* what she taught us. Her arms, her positions, her exactness. But to speak about her system or method, I personally do not undertake it." Osipenko explains further:

> When I was studying, a student from Hungary, Nora Krasotka, came and joined our class. She was a real beauty and a very good dancer. It was very rare for foreign students to join our school at that time. Agrippina didn't leave the Soviet Union, they wouldn't let her . . . well maybe she was allowed to, but she didn't leave. And Nora really pleased Agrippina Yakovlevna. We noticed that during the lessons, in turns, for example, Nora didn't turn like we did under Agrippina Yakovlevna. We did pirouettes at that time with the leg at *coup de pied*, and that's how it is written in her book. *Chaîné* turns we did on *demi-pointe*. Lots of things were like that.
>
> When Nora came, we saw that she turned beautifully, in pirouettes she kept her leg in a high *retiré passé*, and her *chaîné* turns were done *en pointe*. Agrippina Yakovlevna was a very wise person and

she understood that maybe her authority was put under question, but nonetheless she came to the lesson and said, "Today we're going to try to do *chaîné* on pointe." The next class she said, "We're going to try to turn, not with the leg at *coup de pied*, but at *passé*." In other words, she also changed her system over the years. Truly, she could have written a second book of her own.

So for that reason, to speak of her system and method of teaching, she tried to incorporate everything that she saw around her. Seeing something new, she would immediately take it into consideration, and adopt what she considered beautiful and better; therein lay her genius. Now all of us pedagogues, "We are the most 'genius.'" No. She was the brilliant pedagogue.

Gabriela Komleva believes that the basic foundation of Vaganova's method is being preserved. "Time leaves its stamp everywhere, and the same applies to the School. Of course time changes things, and that's normal because things can't just stay in place, and not progress." She explains:

> The basic foundation is still there. Now, however, I am observing a process taking place all over the world, and that is the unification of various schools. The work of other schools is now more available to see. On the one hand this is good, but on the other hand the boundaries are disappearing. It is the natural course of things, and some of the individuality and special traits of specific techniques are disappearing. As happens in other professions. It is a mutual influence. On the one hand the system is being enriched, and on the other hand, you lose something.

As long ago as 2001, Komleva noted these shifts in an article she published in the Vaganova Academy's publication, *Vestnik*. She explained how the Khrushchev thaw of the late 1950s and early 1960s, when political relations warmed between the Soviet Union and the United States, first exposed Soviets to Western art and culture. Later, under Vinogradov (artistic director of the Kirov Ballet during the 1980s and early 1990s), "our ballet was unambiguously oriented to Western values," and that was when the "contours of academic classical dance even for us lost stability and certainty." Nonetheless, Komleva believed that contact with outside influences was necessary. "The point of my article was not to blame the past. It is more important, in my opinion, . . . to respect what is undoubtedly valuable, what was accumulated during the generations of predecessors in the art of classical dance in Russia. It is completely unnecessary to fence ourselves off from the entire world and from the dance culture of the West. We can learn a lot from our foreign colleagues, and at the same time preserve what was discovered in the established [heritage] of Russian ballet as unsurpassable and eternal in the treasury of humanity's spiritual wealth."[12]

That loosening of strict ties to Russian ballet's own heritage is of utmost concern to others who also knew the way things were in the past. Galina Kekisheva is adamant in her belief that the tradition is being lost, and she doesn't find the current situation a pleasant one. "Today it is all disintegrating: everyone at the Academy says that they teach the way Vaganova did. They are trying to maintain it in the school, but it isn't turning out to be good enough."

Kurgapkina agrees with this point of view and believes little remains of Vaganova's method. As she shares her opinions in the pedagogues' dressing room, her voice becomes loud and insistent. "It is all a bit broken now," she explains:

The Mariinsky Theatre is the continuation of the Vaganova Academy. All that is taught in the school is repeated here in the theater every day. Every morning the entire troupe takes class. Earlier, when I was still dancing, we had a separate class for ballerinas. For a time I taught that class, the class of perfection. Of course I consider it a great loss that this sort of class no longer exists. Now, whoever wants to take a certain company class goes and takes it. Men take class from women teachers, and vice versa, and it shouldn't be that way. Ballerinas should have their own class, a special class, a harder one with more pointe work. Now they don't even have classes on pointe. It's very strange but it is a fact.

As for today's pedagogues, both Kekisheva and Kurgapkina insist on Vaganova's strict standards. They say they do not alter what they were taught years ago as students. Rather, they pass it on to the younger generation and hope it takes root. As Kurgapkina points out,

The "method" of ballet itself has existed for 200 years already: fifth position, turned-out knees, arches that neither cave inwards nor pull back, coordination of the legs and arms and head together, that is Vaganova, what she understood very well and what she taught very well. From the beginning everything is done to music, but before you begin any movement, Vaganova said that you have to breathe, the entire body breathes. Unfortunately this method is being violated now, they are breaking it.

Kekisheva laments the recent shift in focus to technique. "Now, the young dancers come into the theater, and they can all do *fouetté*; they can all do large jumps and turns on a diagonal, but then the task of the school was to teach you *how* to do it. Here now the young dancers come, and do it their own way."

At that time, there was only one method. If the movement of the wrist and the head was done like *this*, then *everyone* did it that way. Vaganova attended different classes and very strictly attended to the method, ensuring the fulfillment of one unified method and the singular style of the Kirov Ballet. You could see it immediately, the Kirov [Mariinsky] style, and tell it apart from others.

Now I watch TV and, until I find a face that I know, I can't say what troupe is dancing. They dance well, they dance strongly, they all have long legs and well-arched feet, but they all do the movements a bit differently, especially the arms.

Under Vaganova, the issue was what was the movement done for? *Grand jeté* was for the hip joint. *Rond de jambe en l'air* was for the development of the meniscus.

Kekisheva's words underline the fact that ballet's physical lexicon has never been simply arbitrary. The barre exercises prepare certain joints and muscles in isolation, slowly building to a full-body warm-up. Vaganova noted in her textbook the correct execution of this step that Kekisheva mentions.

Rond de jambe en l'air is a very important movement; it plays a serious role in the ongoing classical training of the body. It must be executed precisely, without allowing the leg to move in the knee joint, as during execution the leg then cannot get the full benefit of the exercise. The correct execution of *rond de jambe en l'air* keeps the upper part of the leg strong and the lower part (from the knee to the foot) obedient in all of the expressive movements, for example, in *fouetté en tournant*.[13]

Kekisheva further elaborates on this detail.

Today the *en l'air* isn't important, they do the step using the whole leg and whole thigh. When I coach the variation of the Fairy of Boldness from *The Sleeping Beauty*, I can barely get anyone to perform the double *rond de jambe* properly. Only with great difficulty do I manage to get them to do it. When our generation—even the generation before us and the one just after us—when we danced, there was no problem. I even rehearsed this variation, I coached it, and the girls came and did it as it should be done. Now they dance it with the whole leg. Instead, the thigh must be held and the lower leg has to be used in isolation. That is just one specific example.

If Vaganova set the preparation for an exercise with the head here, and the hand here, the development of small movements, big movements, everything was thought of. First *tendus* then *battement tendu*; everything was slow and built steadily up to the next steps. You very rarely did *battement tendus* with a high arm. Only later in the center do you do adagio with more expansive gestures. Now they come and do *battement tendu* with the arm high, past the ears, almost past their heads. But if the wrist is here [she lifts her arm directly above her head to an incorrect position, for it is too far back] how can you look at it? Everything is connected.

The dancers today are prepared technically and physically, but not methodically. The *united* method of the school no longer exists. I am upset about this because unnoticeably, slowly, Vaganova's method is dissipating, and working in the classical repertoire has become more difficult.

Now it seems unimportant in the school if the dancer stands on his or her leg properly pulled up, or sits back into the hip socket. What is important to today's dancers is that the *arabesque* is higher than the head. There is no low *arabesque* that maintains a beautiful line, an arabesque from which, for example, you can do a turn. When you're sitting back on the [joint of the standing] leg, you can't go anywhere from there.

Irina Trofimova, now eighty-two years old, still teaches at the Vaganova Academy. Having been selected specifically by Vaganova to study the finer points of teaching, Trofimova is a unique individual whose depth of knowledge needs to be preserved for future generations. Trofimova confirms that the method itself is not and should not be stagnant, but the style should remain unaltered:

Vaganova absorbed anything new that came—Fokine, Duncan. She tried to keep ballet moving forward over time. She changed the approach to this or that movement while we worked with her—a higher *retiré passé* for example, or a higher *coup de pied*. She changed things when young balletmasters' work seemed to require it. And even today, the method is changing, we continue to move forward, we take something even from acrobatics, or use greater flexibility. But it is important not to lose the soul, the musicality and the expression.

While there is little evidence that Vaganova directly incorporated elements of Duncan in her method, we have already seen how she considered any development in dance and evaluated its usefulness: she tailored lessons, at one time, to the acrobatic choreography of Lopukhov, and introduced the higher *retiré passé* of foreign students. Written records as well as the stories of those who knew her confirm that Agrippina Yakovlevna was open to change, that she adapted her method to the influences of the time. Trofimova continues:

Unfortunately with time everything is changing, Vaganova's style itself is changing. I don't want to slander the directors of the Academy, but what is happening is not correct. Tuintina, the pedagogue, worked and lived a long life and she recalled lots of Vaganova. Of course you can modernize some things, but keep the basic style. Tuintina preserved lots of variations, like Fokine's *Armide* on full pointe. But Altynai [Asylmuratova] changed the choreography; she changed the arms. Fokine did not recognize classicism. He was an artist, and now the balletmasters are not artists. There is no artistic direction in the theater. Now ballerinas do it as they want. [Konstantin] Sergeyev did not allow you to change the choreography. The movements, the style is changing with time.

We need to develop the methodology yes, but without losing the style, and that is a very delicate issue. Because after the iron curtain fell, all of the English critics found the nuances in our dance, the soul that we incorporate into ballet; this was a revelation to them. Because at the time the West was only dry form in dance. Now the West has taken a lot from us. And here now there is no sort of image or characterization left.

In terms of methodology, surprisingly, Trofimova was one of the few individuals who belonged to the aforementioned Department of Methodology instituted at the Academy in Vaganova's time. Trofimova describes the processes involved in this office:

I recall that under Sergeyev's directorship, we would have meetings every two months to discuss the specifics of technique and method. We would argue various points. For example, at the time, *chaîné* turns were done on half pointe in sixth position, the legs parallel. Kurgapkina wanted them done in third position, Shiripkina wanted them in fifth. I teach *chaîné* in third position now. You can do them in first, but then the legs tend to separate. Zubkovskaya wanted them in sixth position and Tarasova also wanted them done in sixth.

A theme at one of our meetings was the participation of the arms in the exercises. We would take *temps lié*, for example, and Sergeyev said often, "Let's come to one decision and keep it a unified school." He was very intent on solidifying the methodology, not having various approaches but one single approach. Just as Vaganova had wanted.

We were sent to go look at certain classes, observe them, and report our findings. I checked the middle classes and then would say "you need to pay attention to this and that step."

Later, Kostrovitskaya was invited to Moscow. They adopted lots of our methodology there. The Minister of Culture at the time directed our theater; that was decades ago when the government cared about ballet. In Moscow there were ballet seminars for people from different cities. One was on the training of students from the middle classes in the school. Leningrad—that is, our Academy—was to offer examples of adagio combinations at the seminar, and Moscow would do the jumps. They told me I would go to the seminar and provide these examples. So I took one student each from the fourth, fifth, and sixth classes [or years] in school. I created a small adagio that began with a *grand plié* and went up to *retiré passé* for the fourth year students. I did the same thing, but into a single pirouette from the *plié* for the fifth year students. And for the sixth year, it was a double pirouette. So the technique builds on itself. We presented the combinations and the seminar went well. Peskov, a great Moscow teacher, showed the jumping combinations. The director asked me to give a lecture as well. And at the end we discussed everything.

This sort of theoretical approach seems lost today. There is no more discussion of technique or method.

Altynai Asylmuratova, director of the Vaganova Academy since 2001, contends that the School continues to practice the rigorous methodological reviews established by Agrippina Vaganova, and discusses her perspective at the end of this chapter. A peek inside the Vaganova Academy classrooms supports her claim: things appear remarkably similar to decades past, with rows of perfectly pointed feet and carefully positioned arms illustrating academic positions just as they appear in Vaganova's textbook. The ideal bodies of young girls perform *port de corps* in unison, bending backward until their heads touch their knees. Their legs draw back into high, straight arabesques. Even before their course of training is complete, the students' synchronicity impresses just as much as their beauty; each seems a miniature ballerina in her own right. At least among today's students, despite these pedagogues' harsh words, it appears that much of Vaganova's tradition still remains. It is clear that these pedagogues' commentary comes from a higher plane, underscoring the degree of perfection expected at the Academy, the importance of its style, and the depth of the tradition they insist must continue to be preserved.

A Shift in Aesthetics

"There is a strong tendency now to lift the leg very high," Kekisheva declares.

Her point is one of great contention in ballet circles today, and refers not only to practices at the Mariinsky, but in ballet schools and companies worldwide.

> You know there must be aesthetic, beautiful lines. For example, let's take the Lilac Fairy's variation. Emotionally, given that music, you want the legs to be high, but not just thrown up there into the splits. The music calls for a sharp increase emotionally. All of the method must be preserved, and then you *also* need a high leg. Because at ninety degrees it doesn't look good anymore, you want it to be higher—but not at the expense of the spine or an improper head position. Insofar as, and as much as the style and correctness of the hands and head are preserved, the preparation, that's how much the leg can be lifted. But not for the sake of showing that you can do the splits. And most importantly it needs to be combined with the emotional element of the number or the variation or the performance. If the height of the leg destroys the line, and if it doesn't present an emotional expression . . .

Kekisheva refers to the leg in *écarté*. Vaganova's method explains the pose of *écarté* as follows: "*Écarté* Back. Standing on the right leg, lift the left to *developpé* at ninety degrees toward point six in the classroom."[14] Discussion of a leg above ninety degrees in *écarté* is not given. This is not accidental. Delving further, for her description of grand battements, or "leg kicks," Vaganova prescribed the movement at ninety degrees for beginners, and stated that the "pedagogue must hold back those whose individual capabilities and composition allow the leg to easily reach 135 degrees. (Only) the masterful artist can choose the height of leg."[15]

Kurgapkina provides further background on this phenomenon:

> Agrippina Yakovlevna said that high legs are from the circus, and even those who could lift their legs that high, she did NOT permit it. For example in *grand rond de jambe en l'air*, she told us to lift the leg to the front ninety degrees; at the side, closer to the arm in

second; and to the back the leg can be a bit higher. They lift the leg to the side in *écarté* now, when all of the area "down there" is open to kingdom come; that was considered artistic gymnastics, or even just gymnastics, and, simply put, that was not permitted. I personally maintain the opinion that when *The Sleeping Beauty* stands like a fiancée in *écarté*, and that place is so visible, well, frankly speaking, it is not proper. It is not for classical ballet.

Those who do it now, they probably think, "she's gotten old, that Kurgapkina, she doesn't understand, she could never lift her leg that high." But we had a dancer like that, Galina Pirozhenaya, and she had that sort of extension like they have now, she could do it too, but she did not lift her leg that way. Agrippina Vaganova taught us that it was forbidden. But Galina could do it.

Osipenko has observed the same phenomenon in her dancers at the Mikhailovsky Theatre:

You know the question is difficult and the answer is also difficult. Because now the technique has really increased. If before, my God, Dudinskaya, when she did thirty-two *fouettés*, then it was a gift of fate that you could turn thirty-two *fouettés*; but today they're turning doubles and triples and various tricks . . . the technical execution has increased. But . . .

Osipenko pauses to reflect.

But. . . . Another technique has disappeared: small movements, small footwork, quick transitions, some beauty. Somehow it has all become more monotonous. Footwork has almost completely disappeared in contemporary dance. It is a shame because then the technique lies in something else. Very often I tell the dancers, "Why do you do these miracle technical tricks? Do a very quick 1,2,3 and then hold in arabesque," because that is more difficult. They can turn and turn, and their legs are past their head, that is what you see today; a completely different aesthetic has come to ballet. It is very difficult to persuade them of technique in all understandings and appearances of the term, and not just in turns and jumps. All different kinds of technique can exist.

Tatiana Terekhova underlines this last idea with a short demonstration in the hallway. "Technique is not about high legs," she explains. "Look at this, a fast *pas de bourrée*." She rises from the couch on which we're seated and, legs a blur of motion, performs a crisp, clean rendition of the step on half pointe in her flexible teaching shoes.

That is also technique, but they can't do it now. Technique isn't about that [leg height]; the most difficult technique is in the small movements, and it almost doesn't exist anymore. The dancers today, they simply remove the approaches that aren't comfortable for them.

Of course it's difficult! I'm sorry, but when your legs are by your head, of course it is difficult to attend to the little details. I mean, of course they're easier to do when you have a normal length of leg. I don't have especially long legs, I have proportional ones, but I managed, and for me it was an issue of honor, to dance what I was given, but I had a different task, to execute what was given me, and if I didn't do a certain step, well, that wasn't even an option. I just did it.

"But now for them if it is difficult," Terekhova continues. "Eh," she shrugs, mimicking the dancers' reactions, "and they aren't going to do it. Of course, maybe there's some sort of seed or key in that they have such long legs, and for them some things are more difficult. Specifically from a visual point of view, the ballerinas are longer now. You've noticed this haven't you? They're different, purely aesthetically: they're longer than they were decades ago. So you have to teach them some things. Those elements will also disappear from the technique, if you don't teach them."

Alla Osipenko points out the difference between the Russian and French schools in recent decades:

When Nureyev was still dancing, he invited me to teach at the Paris Opera. He said, "You know Alla, I have this dream that there will be French legs and Russian arms." Since his comment, I also dreamed of this because the French have much worse arms than we do, but they give huge significance to their feet, they have speaking feet, turned out feet, beautiful arches, their feet are like our words, as if they speak with them. Agrippina Yakovlevna gave that same depth of meaning to the upper body. So if that combination had happened, then, it would have been a very interesting influence.

It should be said that foreigners, those same French, they very quickly adopted some of our [Russian] steps. When I was with Moscow's Stanislavsky Theatre in Paris in the 1950s, the Parisians saw the Soviet ballet for the first time. For example, they saw our high lifts and our fishdives . . . unfortunately in everything we were ahead of the entire planet during the Soviet years; for that reason we didn't really look to see what they had that was good. They took a lot from us; they didn't have partnered lifts then, only partnering on the ground. For that reason the French legs and Russian arms.

But is the style of the Russian school still developing? No, it seems to me some pedagogues teach the arms better to their students, some worse. But I think now nothing really moves ahead very strongly, not the way that Vaganova wanted to see.

In an article published in the Vaganova Academy's *Vestnik*, in 2001, Oleg Vinogradov's directorship was imputed as the advent of the changing aesthetic within the Kirov Theatre, a shift that, arguably, damaged the quality of dance. Komleva writes:

Modern choreography with its rush to depart from the traditional form, naturally breaks the classical canon. The precise form of the classical canon has begun to be washed away with the big amplitude of high leg lifts. The use of the step's maximum possibilities cannot avoid affecting the performance of classical choreography. Until the 1960s, the aesthetic of the canon of classical dance demanded that the dancer construct poses in which the torso aspires to a vertical position on the standing leg, allowing the working leg to execute independent movements. Upon lifting the working leg even higher, the possibilities of the hip joint increase at the expense of the supporting leg, [and] the torso loses the advantage of the vertical position due to the compensatory position of the pelvis and spine. Due to this, the turnout of the supporting leg is considerably limited when executing movement.

In the course of twenty years, the former head balletmaster of the Mariinsky Theatre, Oleg Vinogradov, encouraged the dancers to perform movements with the working leg at a specific height. . . .

In our opinion, this was a mistake on the part of the directorship of the Mariinsky Theatre: it is necessary to cultivate the tastes of the spectator, and not to follow in the wake of those who see ballet as a sports competition.

The qualifications of ballet artists include not only complex professional knowledge and practice, but artistic training, which becomes high art at the peak of its execution. Inherent in the understanding of "artistic training" is a level of professional knowledge and practice in which the dancer acts in accordance with aesthetics and taste. The training of taste is formed in the first days of ballet class. Each student's movements are controlled from start to finish, literally by a centimeter of the elapsed distance of the working leg or arm, creating—*training* the same aspiration in the student to comply with the aesthetic canon of classical dance. It is not necessary to substitute expressiveness, birth of the soul, mannerisms, mincing manners or false airs. Artistic training is based on the natural coordination of the person, helping them to overcome everything that is superfluous in movement. Coordination doesn't tolerate inexactness in movement: if imprecision arises, it ruins the execution.[16]

Criticism about the loss of beauty is one reason higher legs and the advent of more "gymnastic" type positions are frowned upon. Concerns about overwork and injury through overtraining is another. Perhaps surprisingly, this topic is not only a phenomenon of the twenty-first century in Russia. Lopukhov wrote of it as long ago as 1937:

I don't want to offend any of the teachers of dance. However I've come to the opinion that they've not pondered the tight dependence of their profession on the anatomy of the individual person. It is not surprising that not in one choreographic effort can I find an answer to my questions . . . In all the books, the movement follows from the point of view of use for the art of choreography—in classroom exercises and in rehearsals. Nowhere is the physical individuality of the person taken into account. Here it is appropriate to ask the question: what exactly is the capability to dance? After all, dance consists of movement which is executed by the ligaments, muscles and even the bones, and the diapason of movement depends on this [interaction] as it "allows" or "disallows" perform-ing some of these movements. Of course much else plays a role. . . .

I don't want to offend the followers of Vaganova, as they are called, and throw a shadow on the method of Vaganova herself, whom I have always called an intelligent pedagogue, a professor of her métier. But I believe that her followers approach her method dogmatically. There is no bad intention in their work but, capti-vated by the talented student, they overestimate his physical capa-bilities or simply do not think of them, based on my own observa-tions. After all, what is helpful and safe for one person can have tragic consequences for another. I, for example, consider N[atalia] Dudinskaya to be a "tough" ballerina; . . . her stamina is unique. And naturally, the work that she could endure would seem harmful to many other people.[17]

Stamina and strength are issues that dancers must contend with on a daily, even hourly basis; overwork can indeed lead to injury. Both Lopuk-hov and today's Mariinsky pedagogues disapprove of overworking danc-ers (see "A Faster Pace" later in the chapter). Today's pedagogues are also disquieted by the increasing leg extensions they see, mainly because the higher positions risk destroying the laws of harmony in movement that Vaganova so carefully defined in her system. Yet the twenty-first century audience appreciates higher legs, and changing preferences over the de-cades have made greater leg extensions not only de rigueur, but even necessary for the aspiring ballerina who wants to remain competitive.

A recent Italian study by E. Duprati in affiliation with Covent Garden demonstrates that the acceptable aesthetic from the audience's point of view has changed over time. That shift has brought with it a trend of higher legs with minimal modification to the position of the torso, which still remains as upright as possible. From Kurgapkina, we know that dancers as far back as sixty or seventy years ago had the same physi-cal capabilities as those today. Therefore, loose joints, flexible arches, and high extensions are not simply creations of modern-day training. The positions we see onstage are a result of a shift in the accepted aesthetic of ballet today and audience preference. Duprati wrote:

For example, the dancer in *Figure 2c* produced an elevation of 96 degrees in 1962, while dancers in later productions increased the elevation to 115 degrees, in 2004. But the same dancer, shown in another position in *Figure 2a*, was physically capable of achieving an elevation of 137 degrees. This suggests that the lower elevation in the first case represents an artistic choice, rather than a physical limitation.

The linear trend shows that variations in body position are systematic, not random. Interestingly, although we specifically monitored leg elevation angles, the trend clearly involves the global visual shape produced by the posture. Indeed, dancers have not

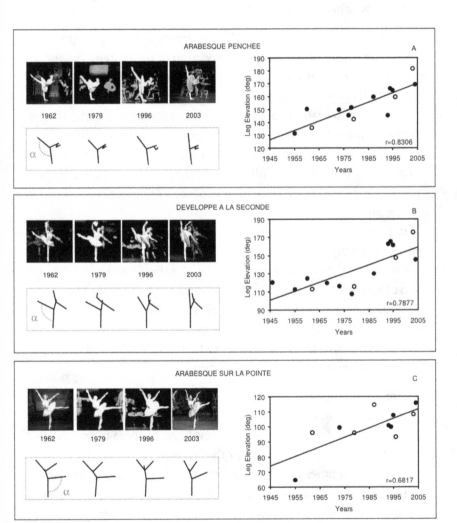

Duprati study, figure 2.

simply aimed at progressively increased leg elevation per se. That could be achieved by a corresponding change in trunk inclination, but we found no evidence for changes in trunk position. Rather, the dancers appeared to perfect the biomechanics of the movement, perhaps by increasing hip turnout, and consequently the range of movement of the working leg. This achieved the characteristic vertical bodyline of recent productions, without modifying trunk position. From this pattern of evidence, we conclude that the variation in leg elevation is an example of progressive, systematic change within an artistic tradition.[18]

However, as Osipenko and Terekhova already noted, leg height alone, or even the nature of the technical execution of ballet steps, do not address the full scope of what is meant by the phrase "Vaganova tradition." Terekhova is one of few pedagogues who has worked extensively outside Russia. Her observations during her time abroad give additional perspective to the issue of Vaganova methods and their preservation.

"They are trying to preserve the Vaganova tradition while the students of Agrippina Vaganova are still alive, at least. Now it is the students of those students who teach, a succession of sorts is happening, a continuity," she says.

"It is very visible when you spend a few years abroad and come back, you immediately think, 'Thank God, here there is still something to look at.' In our theater, the corps de ballet was always very good. Now of course there is a big shift in its level, but all the same they try to preserve the continuity of tradition. They try, of course they try, or it would not have lasted this long; it would have disappeared already."

She believes that the main difference between American dancers and Russian dancers is the level of education:

Here in the Vaganova Academy they teach not just classical dance, but character dance, which is practically not taught anywhere else in the world, maybe only in Germany. Further, there is duet class [pas de deux] which is taught for the last three years of education, regularly two times per week, and at the end there is an exam. Additionally, there is an acting class, a separate subject in which they teach you the dramatic execution of a role. And further, music— playing an instrument such as the piano. So this selection of special

Tatiana Terekhova points out that today the Mariinsky corps de ballet is still "something to look at." The roots of their uniform synchronicity stem from the traditions of Vaganova Academy training. Photo: Stanislav Belyaevsky.

subjects—and I'm not even talking about their classes in the history of ballet, of theater, of music—this is all part of the education. They have a different, higher level of education purely in their own profession.

Then again, we differ in the nuances. There, in America, they don't give the students anything. If you give the children something to do, you show them a step: do you stand this way, or that way? [she demonstrates a position] Is there a difference? Yes, there is. These are nuances that only a Russian pedagogue can give. It looks very expressive when you execute it properly.

In the West that kind of attention is not given. I mean in America. Yes, they have very strong techniques, but there is an absence of the understanding of aesthetics, in my view. A ballerina with short legs, a large, tank of a girl, that kind of dancer does not exist here. A ballerina must have long legs at least, long arms, and be slender. In America, there is a struggle with this aesthetic. I mean a full barrel cannot go out on stage and wear a white tutu and dance Odette. But for them in America, it's normal. There is that automatic, "Put on the tutu and go out there," they are completely fine with it. It's a different level of aesthetic. But they don't allow that here. Here everyone must always be in shape, and the shape, the body, is a very specific type. They choose the children for the school according to certain parameters, there is an index against which they measure the children. The standards are different.

The precise positions and perfect form achieved by Vaganova graduates are the results of years of study. Vaganova Academy graduate (class of 2011) Kristina Shapran is shown here. Photo: Stanislav Belyaevsky.

Indeed, the issue of political correctness as it drives policy in the United States, not discriminating against body types in an art form that is founded on aesthetically pleasing proportions and physical beauty, is handled differently in Russia. In America, it isn't economically feasible for ballet schools to turn away students with less than ideal physiques; and in professional companies there is a higher tolerance for a range of body types, heights, and weights. But at top Russian schools such as the Vaganova Academy, or the Moscow Choreographic Institute, which "feeds" the Bolshoi Ballet company, rigorous selectivity is part of what maintains the uniform "look," and supports the arguably higher Russian standards in this elite art form. A specific body type is sought during the children's auditions each fall for the Vaganova Academy. Genetics and future height and weight predictions are taken into account. It is not unusual for children to be turned away due to something as seemingly trivial as ears that are too large.

Within Russia, the style of dancing in decades past and that of today is another issue. Terekhova continues, "Yes, there is a difference," she laughs, hinting that the answer is obvious. "A huge one. Yes. The dancers today are very capable physically, capable in a way perhaps that we were not. But we danced better, we *danced*. We didn't just do it, we didn't just execute the steps, we *danced* it. Therein lies the difference." Terekhova's words gain emphasis as she speaks, further explaining:

Unfortunately that difference, if you look at the videos, is now developing very clearly. Yes, of course we also jumped and turned, but for us the focus wasn't on putting the leg near the head, you had to create the image, the character.

Now, in any case, until recently, they welcomed purely physical execution—but that's what you learn for 8 years in school! You have to do it; your profession *requires* you to execute the two pirouettes. But it is about the relationship by which you do it, how you do it, and what the part is, so that *Don Quixote* differs from *Swan Lake*.

If you look at a dancer today, if you turn off the music and imagine the dancer without a costume, you will not even guess what they're dancing. The selection of movements everywhere, whether it is *Sleeping Beauty* or *Don Q* or *Corsaire*—it is all done the same way. *The same.* It is the unification of the ballet language. It is now oversimplified. We do what we can. What we know how to do. But the context has been lost. Context has fallen aside. Imagine rewriting Shakespeare in your own words. Can you imagine doing that? I can't. But then why is it done in ballet? What Petipa did was wonderful, and the way they've defamed him now is awful; they've bastardized him, and it's terrible that *that* Petipa doesn't remain. Only one person remains from that era: Gennadi Seliutskiĭ. Oh the headache. We have to struggle constantly.

Gennadi Seliutskiĭ, a warm, fatherly figure to many of his pupils, is a renowned dancer and esteemed Mariinsky pedagogue. Although his dancing years were brief due to injuries, he shared the stage with ballet greats such as Rudolf Nureyev and Yuri Soloviev during the 1960s. Born in 1937 and armed with a wealth of knowledge from decades of experience, he carries himself in a way that suggests the nobility of the Mariinsky stage in years bygone. Since 1963 he has taught morning classes as a professor at the Vaganova Academy, racing back to the Theatre to lead rehearsals with some of the company's finest male dancers.

Seliutskiĭ himself has rather open views about Vaganova's method.[19] "If you watch a film, the form is cleaner nowadays. Method, as I have often said, cannot be unchanging, it is a living thing, constantly developing, but the basics must not be forgotten, this is my opinion. And if the basics are preserved, then the pedagogue can go further and develop the method. We often develop a method further, and lose the basics in the process. We need to look at Vaganova's book and not forget what is written there."

Seliutskiĭ rises from the couch and offers an example. Standing as if at the barre, he says, "For example, *rond de jambe à terre* should be done with the leg moving further out from the body. I ask my students, 'where does the leg begin?' They say 'here,' and point to the hip joint. I say, 'No, it begins here, up near the waist.'" He pulls up straighter and does several *ronds* on the floor, immediately becoming several inches taller, revealing decades of knowledge in several small movements. "If you do it this way, the leg is longer, and you should be reaching out from the body with each *rond*. There are lots of details in her book that we should not forget as we develop the method further."

Gennadi Seliutskiĭ in the role of Albrecht, from *Giselle*. Among his other talents, Seliutskiĭ is known for his great acting abilities. Photo: Mariinsky Theatre Archives.

Seliutskiĭ offers another example, explaining how the shifts in technique have led to new approaches in the classroom. "Earlier they thought that stretching before class would decrease the jump, and it was not recommended. Now the dancers come before the morning class and stretch for twenty minutes or more; they prepare their muscles. This is part of the development of those qualities that are now necessary in modern ballet theater; earlier they were not required."

Seliutskiĭ also has his own views about the tendency toward higher legs in today's performers:

> In terms of today's aesthetics, the human eye quickly adapts to what is new. If you do a *developpé* at 180 degrees and the leg is turned out and the foot pointed, it's beautiful. Like Sylvie Guillem first did it. But I think in classical lessons, dancers need to do it at 90 degrees as well. It is much easier to heft the leg up to 180 degrees, much easier than keeping it at 90. But the form and the beauty need to be preserved; that is the most important thing. However, of course when the eye becomes used to high legs and then someone does 120 degrees, it seems somehow . . . inadequate. It all depends on how it looks, how the form itself is preserved, how the step is executed. You can lift the leg high with beauty and taste, with a beautifully pointed foot. The feet are very expressive parts of the body, they're like hands in speech. The wrists, the head and the feet are three points that are very important, and they can put an accent on any pose.

Trofimova comments on the issue of leg height as well:

> There are higher legs now, yes. And if they're not too high, then it's not too bad. That's fashionable now. Vaganova didn't tolerate it, especially to the side, in *écarté*. She would say, "put your cantilever down," referring to the girls' legs as if they were those beams that signal the arrival of a train on the railroad.

Komleva notes that the difference between today's performers and those of the past, however, is not simply one of technical performance. "Of course, many people notice the difference, not just here but around the world. What is the difference? The depth of the execution of the level of mastery and artistry. Maybe today the physical traits of the younger generation are better in some sense than they were years ago, but the execution and the depth of the artistry, that was more interesting, it was deeper. There is a sort of energy that comes from the inside of an artist. If it is present, then the performance appears completely different. If it isn't there, then the classical is dead, it is boring."

Emotion and Soul

This issue of theatricality or dramatic expression raises another point. Is something not being taught to today's dancers, or has something fundamental changed in the souls of the new generation?

Osipenko explains that style in the current sense of the word differs visually from what was presented by the ballerinas of Vaganova's era. In a soft tone and clear voice, she says:

What do I mean by style? I am trying to explain it to my girls now too. It is a very professional issue. Vaganova's *port de bras* differed greatly from what is taught now in the Academy. In the first place, there was "stat," the Imperial stature; the Petersburg school and Petersburg ballet were known for that and considered to be in first place, above Moscow. And Vaganova was able to transfer that imperial, tsarist essence to her pupils. Shelest and Semënova had it. So now I try, at least, to preserve that, her style, its own worth on the stage. Because now every person calls themselves a ballerina. She's a ballerina, she's a ballerina. Earlier that didn't exist, a ballerina was a title, just like today you have the title of "Honored Artist of Russia." Then you were a dancer of the Mariinsky Theatre. Agrippina Yakovlevna became a ballerina only a year before retirement, and before that she was only a soloist. So for us now there is a different relationship to the word. When people asked me what I did for a living, I never said, "I am a ballerina." I said, "I am a dancer," and to me that is normal, not some sort of excessive modesty; no, it was normal because we were raised that way.

Maybe this is a bit vulgar, but the "*ballerinstvo*," the sense of decorum today has changed. Yes, there is a ballerina, but they do not carry themselves with grandeur and elegance as Dudinskaya or Vecheslova carried themselves.

Osipenko pauses and lifts herself slightly off her chair, "You no longer see this sense of, 'I'm a *ballerina*' with a strong, proud presence." She demonstrates the aura, her neck becoming longer, her head held with pride as if bearing a crown; her arm opens with a sweeping, regal gesture that reveals the elegant image of a ballerina from the late Imperial era. "That indefinable something in their carriage, in their arms, in their glances, in their presence on stage. That grace, the essence of the ballerina, that is disappearing, unfortunately." She continues:

Now I work with girls here and I'm glad that they believe me when I say that you have to open the soul, that you can express a lot with the soul in the art of ballet. And when I say that execution will become more expressive, people will stop paying attention to whether you turned four or five rotations if you turned them in an emotional state, understanding why you are doing it, why five turns are needed. They're needed because the soul demands it; they are an expression of dance. It seems to me very important that they understand that. And they do; they listen to me carefully and understand what I want—Vera Arbuzova and Irina Perren [both leading soloists] and the others. Maybe it doesn't always succeed, because I work with them very little, but in any case they understand that it is not the end, they don't need to just aim for ten turns but to aim for how they're done, or how you lift the leg. You can heft it up there, sure. But you have to do it so beautifully and elegantly, so that the leg says "I'm so beautiful," and not monotonously, "Well here is my leg; look at how high it is." They listen and they understand that technique is not the goal, not the be-all. So you can combine a different technique, this new aesthetic in dance, along with the soul; of course, it is only beneficial.

From Osipenko's words, it becomes clear how a sense of decorum predominated in the past, on stage as well as in real life. Trofimova believes that soul is missing among today's younger performers:

Vaganova's students were all masters of technique, but technique did not interrupt the dancing aspect of movement, the creation of characters onstage. The ballerinas of former decades, for example, Shelest, Vecheslova, Ulanova—Ulanova was not just a dry, technical ballerina, but an actress. Ballet is theater, a theater art. I'm not speaking about divertissements, but actual ballets—*Swan Lake, The Sleeping Beauty* are based on classical literature; they are not divertissements, and they require characters. Unfortunately today these ballets are treated as divertissements with no characterization; the dancers do not work on imagery and characters.

Is it possible to teach that element of acting? Yes. I watched a certain young ballerina who just debuted in *Swan Lake* here at the Mariinsky. She is beautiful; she does it all technically correctly, there are no flaws, but she is not a trembling white swan; it is not Tchaikovsky.

Vecheslova was an actress herself, and she managed to open up Kolpakova's soul; she pulled the soul out of her in her dancing while she coached her. Russian dance in essence is flight, with soul added to it. It is one thing if you are simply performing a divertissement—fine then, perform it. But if you're dancing a ballet, you have to show the music in the character. When you listen to the music, you can see Aurora or Juliet in the music; their characters are visible through the notes. Even this ballerina I mentioned, she can do it; I have seen her do it as the Lilac Fairy, but she doesn't want to do it. It has to do with a lack of world view, a general lack of culture, a lack of understanding. They don't cultivate this in the theater anymore. The dancer must understand that the dance must include the soul; it's not just technique, that this is part of the character. It's not an issue of the modern ballets taking away the soul from the classics either. Even [Irina] Kolpakova danced plenty of Béjart, and that didn't influence how she danced Aurora.

However, whether every dancer is capable of that added element of dramatic expression and emotional depth is another issue. "Can you pull the drama out of a dancer?" Terekhova answers her own question unequivocally:

No. There are people who are capable of being trained, those who are teachable, and those who aren't. I have understood this for a while now. It is a very big task for the pedagogue to pull dramatic expression out of the dancer, because not all are teachable. There are the talented ones; there are those in whom the talent is lacking, and then there are those in whom there is some sort of internal clamp, when for example something happened in their childhood, or in school, and the person was suppressed somehow, and to this day he or she cannot let it out, cannot express it. Somewhere inside they may feel it, but they externally cannot show it, not physically, and not with facial expression.

It is like any profession—you know, there are people who can sew. Can you sew? I can't, I am afraid that I would cut something off, a finger maybe, I could never be a *couturier*, I would be a terrible one. It's like any profession. You either have the talent for it, or you don't.

Alla Shelest, in her writings, held a similar view:

It is commonly said that Vaganova developed artistry in her students. The understanding of the word "artistry," in my view, applies to the individual qualities of the actor—either they have it [artistry], or they don't. The quality developed by Vaganova among all her students I would sooner call professionalism than artistry. Agrippina Yakovlevna taught us such technical methods as coordination in the changing of positions, which fostered stability in execution, freeing the reserves of technical potential. Upon the use of these methods, artists could level out their God-given inadequacies and display the best sides of their artistic talents.[20]

On the other hand, Terekhova points out that a successful ballerina depends on more than just talent. "Galina Ulanova said that talent is 99 percent work." Terekhova pauses, and then adds, "I agree with her." Terekhova tries to impart to her own students a sense of style above all. "Style—is a very *subtle* thing, very insidious. Style. It is the basic foundation of our Leningrad School."

Kurgapkina agrees that technique alone is not what ballet is about. "Of course a dancer must have clean *fouettés*, clean *pirouettes*, and *piqué* turns. Technique is of course the most important, but without expression the technique alone is not needed by any of us; it turns out to be nothing. So, for example, when I rehearse I spend a lot of time and attention so that when the dancer performs the most technical steps, that she puts expression into it."

Then, given technique and the element of dramatic expression, what exactly makes a ballerina successful? Kurgapkina's answer comes quickly. "You have to be very hardworking. Ballet is a terribly difficult profession, involving complete self-sacrifice: You cannot eat, you cannot drink, you have to sleep a little, at the minimum. You have to have a regime of food and of upbringing and, of course, every day you have to take class and rehearse and prepare new parts, because we have a huge repertoire— *Swan Lake, The Sleeping Beauty, Don Quixote, Le Corsaire, Giselle*—all the ballets are so different; so if the ballerina meets the standard even a little bit, well, then that is good.

"Do you know what dusha [soul] is, in Russian?" Kurgapkina asks. "It comes from the word '*dukh*' or breath, inspiration. You cannot teach it: it is either there inside a person, or not. But the presence of coordination, the expression of the eyes in the poses, for example, in *croisé* you look in the direction of the hands, in *écarté* you look at the floor. Simply speaking, the eyes have a defined position in ballet too. And when the eyes, legs, arms, everything together goes from pose to pose properly, that is the soul, and it is very expressive. And it is music[al] as well."

Kekisheva points out a general difference between past and present generations that, in her view, accounts for the increasingly frequent lack of dramatic expression on stage today. "I see a big difference between the dancers of today and those from the past. I see a huge difference, I see a lot of mechanical execution. They don't manage to dream. A ballet artist *must* dream." Kekisheva smiles, and pauses. "They must go home, lie down, not sleep, but listen to the music, and dream about how they will execute a role. Like this? Like that? They don't manage to do that now. They come to rehearsal and apologize, 'Galina Petrovna, I didn't manage to watch the video, I didn't learn the order of the steps; if it's not too hard, can you teach it to me?' At first I was offended; I was exasperated, and then while I was working, I understood. Another girl said to me, 'this is only my seventh rehearsal, and the first two of them were setting the steps.'"

Kurgapkina agrees. "Yes, there was a difference, and there is a difference. Aside from technical differences, of course. In our time they added mandatory expression. And moreover, the arms were different from each ballet to the next. In *Don Quixote*, for example, hands on the hips. In *The Sleeping Beauty*, the arms went precisely to each position. In *Swan*

Lake, the arms simply breathe along with the head, but if you move only the arms, and the neck and head don't move, it doesn't look quite right. So it seems to me that the taste of ballet has changed. People look at it differently, and ballerinas see themselves differently. It should be like a paint color. Paint is the arms and eyes. Each performance [ballet] has its own color, and that color has to be maintained. Or the costumes. For example, before, the [skirt of the] costume for *Giselle* would never just lie flat against the legs; it was supposed to be separate, off the body, as if it simply happened to fall there, floating."

Gennadi Seliutskii agrees that the element of soul is not as present today as it was in decades past.

> Technique has developed, but the soul? With the soul now, it is more complicated. Though dance, ballet that is based only on form and technique is not to me personally effective. You must have the element of the soul, it is mandatory. And when these two things are combined, then you have real theater. When there is a certain atmosphere, and the person onstage carries the emotion and thoughts forward; he thinks; he relates to his partner, and truly loves her; he isn't just executing steps as they were set, but when he incorporates his condition and his emotions into what he does, that is theater.
>
> Now they often call us a "company" but we are not a company; I don't like to use that word in relation to the Mariinsky Theatre. The term "theater" is a very high-level, specific term. The number of people who can jump and turn today are many, but those you can define as artists are very, very few. Years ago, of course, there was maybe less attention paid to cleanliness of technique, but there was plenty of soul in the dancing, but the time was different then. There were fewer performances than we have in the theater today, and the dancers get more tired [now]. So these conditions, as well as what happens in the world around us, it all influences the quality of the dancing.

Unequivocally, all of the pedagogues agreed on one thing: in order to be successful, a ballerina must first and foremost be hardworking. Kekisheva elaborated on that point:

You can have average physical traits and be a very hardworking person, and you can become a proper dancer. You can have a wonderful body, but if you are lazy, and if your life isn't in the theater, but somewhere else, you will never achieve anything. The ideal combination, of course, is the perfect body and a huge work ethic. Fanaticism, but in a good way. Then you can become a great artist. But you have to live in the theater; it is your life, the theater, the stage. It doesn't matter what level you're at, the corps de ballet or the ballerina. I know some wonderful ballet artists who have very bad work ethics. But in the theater, technique is really a very small part of what we work on: company class is very short, an hour, or an hour and 20 minutes, maximum. I try to teach my dancers accuracy and correctness above all, so that, for example, *petit battement* is done at the ankle and not at the calf level. So that if they do a *developpé devant*, then the *passé* is here.

Kekisheva stands and demonstrates a *retiré passé* in perfect form. "With the foot in front, and not in back of the knee. But to them it's all the same. They come and do a *passé* and lift the leg to the back. How is that possible? If you're lifting into arabesque, [based on the rules of Vaganova's method] the foot goes up the back of the leg. It's as simple as that."

A Faster Pace:
The Twenty-First Century

The need for a scrupulous work ethic in the would-be successful dancer is not just an issue of competition, not simply a requirement of the profession. Kekisheva and other pedagogues agree that the regime inside the Mariinsky Theatre today has shifted and that the faster pace of life in the twenty-first century is partly to blame for what they see as a difference in acting abilities or even technique. The workload has increased: there are more ballet performances per month, the dancers dance more roles more frequently, and there is always a "reserve" troupe that remains in St. Petersburg while the bigger name stars tour to various international cities throughout the year, all evidence that the Mariinsky has moved toward a more global, even "Western" work model.

Indeed the workload of the Mariinsky artists, untouched by the standards of union labor that many Western and European companies must follow, is almost unfathomable. During their eleven-month full-time season, typical working hours are 10 A.M. to 10 P.M. if the dancer is scheduled to perform. It is not uncommon for dancers to use the intermission time during a performance to rehearse another ballet, only racing back onstage to complete the evening's performance. Without union rules that might otherwise limit excessive hours, it is also not unusual for dancers to go weeks, if not months, without a single day off. Designated rest days are more often than not replaced by last-minute rehearsals. Constant touring also takes its toll.

With the increased workload, the time left to address stylistic issues is minimal. While the Mariinsky has adapted to the pace of the twenty-first century, the stress and workload on the dancers is exponentially greater than it was only twenty years ago.

Terekhova comments on this phenomenon, conceding that "they try to preserve the traditions. They are trying. But it seems to me that in the past, the graduates were better prepared stylistically. They were better educated. Now, they dance more and study less. Earlier they studied more, and danced less—I'm speaking about during the school years."

"Practice is needed of course, but there is an unbelievable number of performances now for the Academy's students: they go on tours, perform at the Hermitage Theatre or at a theater in another country, this and that. Maybe this takes up the time that they need to learn, let's say, to dance. It is a huge problem now. The education of those who dance."

If the problem of time is present in the Vaganova Academy, it only worsens once the students join the theater. Kekisheva says, "Working with the dancers now is very difficult. How can we preserve things the way they should be? I am not even sure it is possible to do something about it." She elaborates:

We have rehearsals for a variation for a maximum of 15–20 minutes, and if in that amount of time you have to teach them that, in the approach to *glissade*, the head goes towards the front foot and not the back, time is lost. With us, they didn't have to explain that; we already knew that if the foot is in front, the head goes towards that foot, and then changes. But now they do it any way they want, it's all the same to them. They don't care. They tell me now, "today we don't do it that way." Now there is no true, genuine style. Under Vaganova there was a definite *style* of the Kirov Theatre.

When I was dancing, I worked under the famous ballerina Ludmila Lukom a lot. I did the exercises, and if there was an evening performance she would say to me, "Galochka, go home and rest." I went and rested and came back, with emotion, and I was joyful to be on the stage.

"And now?" Kekisheva asks, imitating a student approaching her, serious and exhausted, "'Galina Petrovna, I have a performance in thirty minutes.' From that morning the dancer had company class, one rehearsal, a second, a third, and in the evening she must dance a solo part." Kekisheva's voice increases in tone, as she insists defensively, "What sort of emotional output can they offer? How can they preserve themselves somehow, in order not to break? For an artist of ballet, if she is out sick for one week, she needs two weeks to return to the shape she was in before the sickness."

As far as the pedagogues are concerned, part of the problem seems to be those doing the teaching. A secondary issue is the expansion of global communications. Outside influences were few and far between 110 years ago. Now, the click of a mouse on high-speed wifi can get you a ballet video from just about anywhere in the world.

"Now there are some pedagogues in the School [Academy] who think they should bring in something new. I call this 'cassette education [teaching],'" Kekisheva explains. "They look around the world and take little bits of something from here and there. That shouldn't be; we need another personality like Vaganova, someone who can be the axis, who can develop things, but keep it all together. Not break it, but develop it."

Kurgapkina notes these influences as well. "Earlier nothing was on video, we didn't have them, so everything was passed from person to person. And Vaganova said, 'Try to learn a role from the person who dances it the best.' This is very important, because the way it is shown to you is the way you are going to dance it. It truly is that way. It means a lot if you like the dancer and she can show you the steps, but now you can watch who dances on television or video. Not long ago they showed ABT's *Le Corsaire* on TV. And now the dancers get everything from the outside, and that isn't for the best."

Tatiana Terekhova agrees that the influx of external information isn't always a positive phenomenon. "Unfortunately. Now there is a great quantity of ballet material that we can watch on TV and computer, but it brings a little bit different taste, and unfortunately many dancers work with the absence of taste today; they do not understand the style that is connected with and rooted only in this theater.

"In this theater you have to dance very cleanly in style. The slight nuances are things that only a knowledgeable pedagogue can give you. Do you look up, or across? Is there a difference? Only the pedagogue can tell you that, because the ballerina can't see it for herself. And then with more global things, for example, four pirouettes, it is clear enough when they have been executed, but *how* were they done, with what *style*, with what *character*, with what *form*? The pedagogue does all of that." Terekhova gives an example of the heavier workload today's Kirov dancers must carry:

When I was performing, I danced the Pas de Trois in *La Bayadère*, and after that they would never have put me in the Grand Pas in the same performance. Never. Now a dancer will be given the Grand Pas and then one of the three Bayadères too. Probably there are lots of reasons why: we have two stages, and a huge repertoire. If, decades ago, the orchestra, ballet, and opera discussed together which performances we could give back to back without disturbing each other, well, now they can easily put *The Sleeping Beauty* and *Raymonda* on the schedule, even on the same day. For example, this weekend we're going to have *The Little Humpbacked Horse* and a gala concert in the same day, two performances, at 12 noon and 7 P.M. But at least [the new deputy director Yuri] Fateyev makes sure that different dancers perform in each performance.

Terekhova shakes her head in mild frustration. "Under [former director Makhar] Vaziev I am sure that it would have been the same dancers. Without question."

Kekisheva echoes these sentiments, expressing frustration at the pace of work inside the theater today.

I would like to see a more fair artistic life. You shouldn't burden the dancers this much; they get broken as artists and become mechanical, and then they enter the stage as different people. For example, we should have three or, maximum four ballets performed per week. It would be better if there were only three, so that there is time to rest, and to "come to" as a human being. Time simply to think about why and how you're going on stage. Now this is the biggest problem. On the one hand it is good because they learn the technique; they get used to the stage; they don't fear the stage as we did. After all, when you perform only three or four times per month, it's frightening! But now it is simply an exhausting excess; it's just too much. It should be so that they have a lot [to do], but so that it doesn't grow into indifferent legwork and footwork. To go out there, dance and then leave. . . . Art without soul is not art. It's true. Please, gymnastics is gymnastics—it's also without emotion.

Kekisheva looks directly at me in explanation, the frustration in her voice audible.

The school's responsibility is to know the *school*, and by that we mean the style and the system that it propagates. The children today do not know the school; they do not study it; they don't have time for it. They themselves are touring and performing!

Time plays a role without a doubt because of the huge number of performances, concerts of the school, even tours of the school, they are endlessly rehearsing.

I know a pedagogue in the school, and she says to me, "I am going to rehearse a little girl the *pas de deux* of *Giselle*." To that I say, "Lusinka, my dear, why not let her do the exercises one extra time! What *pas de deux* of *Giselle*? What are you talking about?"

You see, each pedagogue at the Academy, especially those of the graduating class, considers it necessary to graduate a "ballerina." So a moral or psychological breakdown occurs. There [at the Academy] they tell a dancer that she is a *ballerina*, and she can do this and that; but here in the theater they can't even give her a mark of 4 [a grade B];[21] she professionally cannot cope; her arms, her *port de bras* are incorrect, they're not in front of her head in third high, they're past her head. Almost behind her. It's all very sad. Now it seems to me that the Vaganova method almost doesn't exist anymore. Maybe time is to blame, I don't know.

This difference in what the students are allowed to dance—granting each one a role suited to his or her level of technique—is one main departure from the practices of the past. Kekisheva explains that when she was a student, Vaganova allowed only the best girls in the school to perform a *pas de deux* for the graduation performance. "The best, whether from the provinces or from the city, whether she will later be a soloist or ballerina. The rest were given grades of 4 or 3. Or they might do a special number where there is a pose or a lift. In this way, each dancer's individual talents were celebrated at the graduation performances, but each dancer also had a ceiling, a limit as well."

Kekisheva's observation that perhaps not every dancer should receive a solo at graduation echoes her earlier statements about the trend to create a "ballerina" no matter what. Similarly, Terekhova thinks more oversight should be given to the structure within the theater and how the new graduates' career paths are carved:

> I would like us to have a normal plan of work connected with the development of the students. Dancers grow, but they should develop within the careful framework and observation of the directors, as in the past they prepared us for the stage. That is why our parts were ideally prepared. But I would have to wish our dear company that the dancers will work without sickness and there will not be injuries. The issue is that if you are prepared from the very beginning, from your training, you can do it well, but if not, you cannot. You cannot play catch-up later. But today it's not important what you dance, you're in all four acts.

The Repertoire

The question of methodology reaches into the realm of the theater's repertoire as well. Almost without exception, pedagogues wish the theater would revive some of the gems in its own repertory and, perhaps surprisingly, they attest to the need for new works as well.

"We need a balletmaster who would bring something new to the repertoire, not just form and movement, but a soulful, new ballet with elements of emotion and drama. Right now it is a vacuum," Kekisheva explains.

I enjoyed this new performance by [Alexei] Ratmansky of *The Little Humpbacked Horse* [2009]. It is soulful, inspiring; there's contemporary movement, and even the modern sets didn't bother me. I watched it with pleasure because I saw that a masterful true artist had created it; I enjoyed it even more than his *Cinderella*.

So you need some strong, firm hand that would at a minimum preserve the Vaganova method and not break it. And not simply say, "It isn't important where her arm is; she's standing like a ballerina." What is that, "like a ballerina?" It's tasteless, forgive me for saying so.

I consider that all these modern and contemporary dances, they are necessary; they're part of our times; they [the audience] like it; they're even bored without it, but, again, it has to be done with quality.

Kekisheva offers an example of how impressive modern works can be, when danced well.

Recently, I saw Svetlana Zakharova when she danced at the Gala Concert for Olga Moiseyeva. Zakharova danced two contemporary numbers, and I was truly delighted at how well they were performed, with how much professional taste, and how greatly executed. Then, when she came out in the classical *Don Q*, it wasn't as impressive. I remembered her in the modern piece. So it's necessary. Time goes on, it's necessary. But, if the troupe of the Mariinsky-Kirov Theatre wants to endure, then the Vaganova method must remain steel-willed.

And of course, it seems to me we have to look again at the whole repertoire created during the Soviet period, and not simply adopt everything—take something, but not everything. There are many wonderful ballets by [Leonid] Yakobson. Why do we only have one *Legend of Love*, by Grigorovich? When there are no other balletmasters like him in the world today.

Why must we have some middle-level mediocre productions by others? After all, not all of Balanchine was wonderful, but take the best of his work. Show that we can dance it, that we can dance this, and this. But from *our* repertoire, we should not forget the best of our own creations.

Kekisheva's voice gains a tone of urgency as she discusses the need for reviving old Soviet ballets.

Thank God, now we're going to re-stage Yacobson's *Shurale*. Very few people remain who can completely and valuably restore it, but there are some. There is no reason at all why Yakobson shouldn't be performed here. And there are many such examples. The Grigorovich ballets, and Fyodor Lopukhov's wonderful production of *Spring Fairytale*. Why can't we take something from Vinogradov? He is here now; take his *Knight in the Tiger's Skin*; it has beautiful music. Shorten it somehow, if you like. He's alive and well and here, so use him. It will be much more interesting than what we often present and waste energy on.

There is a debate, however, as to whether other ballets, more modern additions to the repertoire, are harmful to the classical physique so carefully honed through years of schooling at the Vaganova Academy and later inside the theater. The opinions appear to be mixed. Kekisheva, while admitting the necessity of modern choreographic works, is not sure they're safe for the dancers.

You know, I think they harm the physical traits of a person. In classical ballet you have to hold up the spine, you have to incline the torso as much as is allowed without ruining the beauty of the line. Modern ballets have uncontrolled bends, and although they have a class for this at the Academy now, I believe there should simply be defined limits [about what is danced]. Because otherwise, you break the spine, the meniscus is crushed. And they talk about how it is only beneficial—no, it isn't. You have to know, this contemporary balletmaster, can his work be done in a classical troupe or not? Because all of his movements require an atypical sort of flexibility. If a person only does these modern movements, if today he dances this person's work and tomorrow he has to dance Petipa's *The Sleeping Beauty*, and he's still holding himself that way . . . or if after Petipa he doesn't keep up his back and something happens with legs or thighs or knees . . .

I think it's necessary to have the new works, because times change, and people see other things, and they want to try something new. It's all needed. But you have to, first, very clearly understand what you can substitute; you have to see the classics of the Mariinsky Theatre and find contemporary productions that do not destroy the physical capabilities of the classical ballet dancers here. For the classics are the basis, the bones of the Mariinsky Theatre. In order to not ruin that, you need to do the contemporary repertoire in a way that does not physically destroy the dancers, and this isn't always successful.

Komleva is less fearful of the influence of modern movement on the dancers. Commenting on the inclusion of modern works into the repertoire, she says, "Yes, it is wonderful, and it is great that it is even possible. I have to say that the dancer who has mastered classical technique and has that foundation can easily dance modern works, but the reverse path is much more difficult. Those who dance modern well don't necessarily do classics well, because the classics are the most difficult execution for dancers. The demands are greater, the physical form must be good, musicality, knowledge, and intellect too, by the way [are required]. And if that isn't there, it's boring to watch."

"Sometimes it happens that the dancers come out of an athletic contemporary performance and it takes them longer to return to classical shape. But it is possible, and all the same they return. It just suits some of them better. There are just different approaches that exist in different repertoires."

Kurgapkina openly admits that she is "for the classics. Each director wants to have something new in his theater. I, however, am categorically against the fact that these [modern] performances go on. Well, of course once or twice, maybe. But why can't we restore *Shurale*, *The Bronze Horseman*, *Laurencia*, or *The Flames of Paris*? These are our masterpieces, and they are very difficult ballets, very expressive ones. What could be a better place to do them than here? Instead of these modern whippersnapper productions, people jumping around the stage—it's not really dancing," the agitation is apparent in Kurgapkina's voice. "But this is just my taste," she adds, "I don't know."

Trofimova agrees that the theater needs new works, but done in a high-quality manner, and perhaps in the classical mold:

Of course, you want a fresh ballet. Earlier, Petipa would set three to four new ballets each year. We had *The Flames of Paris, Laurencia, The Fountain of Bachchisarai*, all wonderful productions. Fragments of them are still danced. *Othello* and *Cinderella* came after the second World War. And there were a few unsuccessful productions too, perhaps *The Shores of Hope* or [more successful] *Leningrad Symphony*. We also had *The Little Humpbacked Horse* and *The Pearl*, but there were new ballets. Now, they do not set new works, or if they do, the quality is so low that you don't remember the production later.

When Balanchine brought his work back to us, the ballets were form without emotion. But that is his style, he does it his way, and you have to understand it.

But about musicality, Balanchine does not give the upper body much movement. I don't recall the name of the ballet, but at a crescendo in the music, he offered a very small step. With that sort of music, you want to see a big jump or lift. There is no need to confuse rhythm with music. His rhythm was exacting, but musicality in that particular case was lacking. It's not always understandable why he does it, because the culmination in the music doesn't coincide with the culmination in the dance, in some instances. On the other hand, at the time there were no traditions in the United States, so he [initially] did everything in an empty space, and the technique of the dancers there was more primitive [than in Russia], so maybe that's why the steps were smaller, more simple.

Agrippina Yakovlevna was artistic director for a period and she allowed the balletmasters to try new forms. Lopukhov tried to set formalistic ballets. She also set dances. I danced her *Waltz Fantasy*, she was very musical. It is too bad that number is now lost. With Fokine's *Chopiniana* she sensed the stylization there. Now they dance this like a classical ballet, but she maintained its [romantic] stylization.

They say they don't allow the young ones to try, or else they try to stage formalistic ballets of some kind. It isn't clear why. In the past there were so many balletmasters—[Rostislav] Zakharov, [Boris] Fenster, [Fedor] Lopukhov, [Oleg] Vinogradov. Now they are adopting William Forsythe and Balanchine, but what about our own heritage?

Although Balanchine is widely recognized for his musicality, to someone raised on a steady diet of Petipa and Ivanov, where choreographic choices follow logical, sometimes even predictable music-based patterns, the idea of filling a musical crescendo with something other than an expansive gesture—a high lift, for example—is rare. However, the comments from Trofimova and Kurgapkina underscore the role that Russian choreographers have had in the development of ballet worldwide, as well as the importance of preserving the Mariinsky's historical repertoire while also incorporating new works.

Terekhova expands on the loss of some of the Mariinsky's greatest ballets. "We don't appreciate the value of what we have until we lose it. And that is what is happening now. There's no way to restore *The Bronze Horseman*, it had lots of general corps de ballet scenes. The only way would be if the soloists can recall something. It was a wonderful production. We had friends from the Australian Ballet, and they said you could present only that production in Australia and earn tons of money. It is a dramatic ballet. And you need only Leningrad people to dance it."

The late Natalia Dudinskaya shared the same viewpoint:

As for the blind imitation of the West, the so-called fashion, the style of "modern," unfortunately it has no place. It seems to me not all foreign choreographers of the West have professionally mastered the basics of the classics. They grasp at them, studying the Soviet school of classical dance. It is generally known that the birth in France of classical dance reached its genuine peak only in Russia. Classical works can only be set by a true professional.[22]

One Pedagogue, One Ballerina

In the past, the system was different. Ballerinas rehearsed various roles with different pedagogues. If they worked on *Swan Lake* with one person, then their coach for *Giselle* may well have been someone else.

That system no longer exists in the Mariinsky Theatre, and in its place is a pairing up of pupil with pedagogue, with little room for overlap. Not everyone is sure this is a positive state of affairs.

"When I was dancing," Kurgapkina explains, "we had various pedagogues. For example, Lukom rehearsed [dancers in] *Giselle*. Dudinskaya did *Don Q*. The ballerina could change pedagogues, and the pedagogue could choose her ballerina. That is what it was like before. Now, I prepare everything, every role with my girls. And if you leave your pedagogue, it means you leave completely, forever. You don't go back."

Kekisheva doesn't hesitate to share her own strong views on this issue.

I consider what is going on now to be harmful. It came from the ice skating competitions—each trainer with his athlete, and each trainer with his awards. We shouldn't have that. Earlier it wasn't that way. The director decided, "this ballerina would be best to rehearse this ballet with that pedagogue, and the next performance would be better if she worked with this pedagogue." Because each coach can give something of their own to the ballerina.

For example, if as a ballerina you don't have expression, then you have to work with a pedagogue who is very emotional and understanding and who can explain what exactly the meaning is. If you don't have the right technique, then you need a coach who can help you with technique, like a trainer. One pedagogue may give less artistic help but may be able to demand something else from the dancer. It is not a creative system now, because one person can offer a certain kind of help and another can offer something different, and the director should be able to see that among the pedagogues, and define it. Because the circumstances from this [current] arrangement don't turn out to be very nice, and for business it isn't very good. Especially when the dancer is working on individual solo parts.

Not all dancers are good at everything—some are better at certain elements. But now the pedagogues are very possessive. And if a pedagogue is not very determined to put their pupil out there in the limelight, then that student will suffer.

Perhaps I'm wrong. It is interesting when the pedagogue can ignite the dancer from within, and get them to open up. This is a good thing. But it also happens where you don't share the same approach or don't suit each other, and so it seems to me there is something more negative in this current system than positive. This arbitrary assignment is painful when the two individuals are not a good fit. It's possible to do it for a while, but it turns out to be narrow and you begin to see not the artist but the pedagogue on stage; the dancers begin to look like carbon copies, down to the very last detail of the *révérence*. So the student looks just like the teacher.

Kekisheva is not the first to note this phenomenon. Lopukhov spoke of it nearly seventy years ago. As a contemporary of Vaganova's, his view can be taken as representative of some opinions of that era:

The question of copying is a very serious and principal one. I want the balletmaster-*répétiteur* to understand it correctly without additional offense. I have the opposing view—it is better to have a good copy than a bad original. [But] even in the good copy there is no movement forward. . . .

I do not say that . . . dancers can't be balletmaster-*répétiteurs*. Only, for this you must forget yourself and your individuality, and try to see something new in the face of your pupil, which is only possible if you constantly lead them away from copying. It is not easy, and certainly different rehearsal coaches manage to different degrees. For example in Leningrad, N[atalia] Dudinskaya, T[atiana] Vecheslova and S[vetlana] Sheyina are working in the capacity of pedagogues. All of them have not completely "forgotten" to "stumble" upon the past, offering their own interpretations of roles to young artists. It is possible that this happens subconsciously, for the dismissal of oneself is done only with great difficulty. It seems that this happens also because the profession of balletmaster-*répétiteur* is new: after all, in the past not one ballerina of those I remember—not Vazem, not Sokolova, not Kshessinskaya, not Preobrazhenskaya, not Pavlova or Geltser—none worked with others on their roles. They only took ballet lessons.[23]

Lopukhov and Kekisheva's comments underline the perennial issue of carbon copies and the loss of individuality as something that all pedagogues must struggle to prevent.

The Changing Audience

Over a century ago, the St. Petersburg audience was mostly aristocratic. Ballet was an elite art, attended by the nobility. A sense of decorum predominated in the theater. Ballerinas carried themselves with glamour and pride, and the upper echelons of society composed the majority of the Mariinsky-going public. Trofimova points out how the Russian audience shifted with the advent of Communism in Russia:

> Part of Vaganova's merit is that she defended classical ballet during the Russian Revolution. That was her principle, because at the time people cried out that Tchaikovsky is garbage. She wrote articles, attended meetings under conditions of cold and famine. Then in the '20s, after the war, everyone left Russia and headed West, but Vaganova remained and struggled to set the classics. I'm not sure why she stayed, but I think she wanted to build her career here. After the war, another type of viewer came to the theater. No longer was it filled with lovely people dressed in silks and furs, but common folks in boots and overcoats. Nonetheless they loved the ballet.
>
> When Diaghilev's *Russian Seasons* [Les Saisons Russes] showed *Giselle* for the first time, everyone was surprised because in the West, in Europe, the classics had been forgotten until then. Russia preserved the classics. When Balanchine brought his works back to us, the ballets were form without emotion. Even Krasovskaya, the famous Russian dance writer, liked it, this formalism.

It may be difficult for some Soviet-era dancers and choreographers to conceive of emotion in dance apart from narrative and characterization; for them, this element of dance performance seems inextricably

Irina Trofimova coaches a student inside the Vaganova Academy. Photo: Stanislav Belyaevsky.

wedded to the story ballet. Yet numerous choreographers over the decades have created formalistic ballets void of specific story lines, some requiring defined emotions, and some focused more on poses and positions. Not all ballets are based on a specific dramatic message and, in some cases, more abstract works may be easier for the audience to digest.

In the post-revolutionary years, the new audience that Trofimova refers to did not "understand" much of what they saw from the classical repertoire. In an odd continuum, some of the pedagogues interviewed for this book intimate that a similar trend is happening today, especially among younger viewers. They suggest that the advent of democracy in Russia and its related distractions—high technology, or the general culture of consumption—is killing off appreciation for the arts, namely, the classics. The faster pace of the twenty-first century has accustomed youth to the quick fix that the Internet, cell phones, and video games may provide. A higher leg may now be more appealing than a lower leg held in a perfectly academic position—partly because the understanding of academism itself is changing, if not fading. Six pirouettes will be more intriguing to watch than one because *more*, sometimes, is considered better. Now, as decades ago, the general cultural knowledge shared by previous generations may not be as strong as it once was. Komleva still calls ballet an art of the elite. "The new viewers are not always dedicated—you have to love it and be dedicated. Ballet isn't pop culture, after all," she says, "it is also an art that you [as the viewer] have to learn and study."

Russia and Europe as a whole continue to educate children in operatic libretti and basic classical ballet plots to a greater degree than elsewhere. General childhood education has a strong focus on the arts, and exposure to classical music and art history is widespread. In the United States, sports and film—or those arts and pastimes that offer immediate satisfaction and require less preparation on the spectator's behalf—receive more attention.

In the United States, *The Nutcracker* is perceived by most people as a holiday event rather than a ballet theater experience. It is also the single most important fund-raising opportunity for most ballet companies, and it is the only exposure to ballet that many Americans have. In Russia, on the other hand, *The Nutcracker* is performed by numerous ballet companies year-round, not only in December, and it represents a very small segment of most citizens' theater experience.

Thankfully, despite the perceived shift in the younger generation, today a substantial portion of the Mariinsky audience still arrives at the theater well versed in the history of classical ballet, aware of the nuances in a libretto, or the technical feats and faults that they watch onstage. Ballet attendance for them is much more than an annual *Nutcracker* outing. The Mariinsky viewers are dedicated and loyal and, in terms of the traditional classical repertoire, they remain well educated in what they see on stage: they know characters by sight and have much of the choreography already memorized. In fact, in no other theater are the expectations for dancers' debuts on stage as high; in no other hall is the silence during a premiere so unbreakable.

As time stretches further from the founding personalities of this classical art, one fears the connection to its roots may become even more tenuous. But it seems that the handful of pedagogues and ballerinas mentioned on these pages are making a difference by dedicating themselves to the preservation of those old traditions.

Two Petersburg Ballerinas: Lopatkina and Chistiakova

It is one thing to discuss legend and theory but another to see it in practice. Uliana Lopatkina is revered by historians, critics, ballet lovers, pedagogues, and her fellow artists as one of the last representatives of authentic Vaganova style. A purist, workaholic, and perfectionist, her highly analytical, careful approach to her art leaves no room for error. Given the importance of the pedagogue in every Russian ballerina's stage career, it is revealing to learn that unlike others in the company, she has been able to select her coach. And her choice fell on the former soloist Irina Chistiakova.

Chistiakova's dancing was characterized by painstaking attention to the nuances of movement, strength of execution, and strict academism. She has long since retired from the stage, but continues to teach and coach in various places in St. Petersburg. She worked at a school in Italy for two years, taught in Cincinnati for several summers, and has been invited to give master classes wherever the company tours. Moreover, until 2007 she ran her own ballet studio in Petersburg, a school that welcomed professional dancers as well as children and nonprofessionals. "Some come just to touch their childhood dream. Just out of interest and the desire to dance," she says.

Her main focus in the past six years, however, has been Uliana Lopatkina. After a long discussion with the former dancer-turned-coach, and several forays into their rehearsal studio, it becomes clear just what the Vaganova tradition, in practice, means.[24]

"My first exposure to ballet happened when I was 3 or 4 years old,"

Irina Chistiakova as Kitri from *Don Quixote*. Chistiakova's strong technique made even the most difficult roles easy for her. Photo: Mariinsky Theatre Archives.

Irina Chistiakova says "*How* you lift your leg is more important than how high it goes. If you don't have the technical base, that is bad, but if you only have technique, that is also bad. Better to go to the circus if that's the case." Here she is shown with Farukh Ruzimatov in the rehearsal studios, 1985. Photo: Yulia Larionova.

Chistiakova explains. "I watched the ballet *Shurale,* a production by Leonid Yakobson, a fairytale in which the girl is a bird. I also watched *Swan Lake* on TV. Something in ballet attracted me then."

Chistiakova explained her beginnings in ballet the night after I'd watched her coach Lopatkina and Ivan Kozlov in the Mariinsky studios.

When I was five, my mother sent me to study English in a group that school children typically attended, and nearby was a ballet class. One day I passed by the class and watched it. I began to skip the English class to watch the ballet class. I was too young to participate, but I wanted to watch. One day I forgot to leave at the time that the English class normally finished, so my mother came looking for me. She found me watching this ballet class, and the teacher there told her that I had been coming every day to watch it. She told my mother that I was too young still, but to let me watch how the dancers move.

I continued to watch those ballet classes, and soon the pedagogue at the ballet school put up an announcement about a class for younger children, age six. Enough children enrolled, and the class began. But I found it interesting at that point to watch the adult classes too, to see how they moved. So I took my class, and then stayed later to watch the class after me. That pedagogue was a former Mariinsky dancer, and suggested to my parents that they take me to the Vaganova Academy.

My family tried to talk me out of pursuing ballet, saying it was difficult, a hard life, but I went to the Vaganova Academy anyway, and was accepted.

The atmosphere in the Academy then was quite different from how it is now, because I studied with pedagogues who were born in the nineteenth century not the twentieth, and they made a completely different impression on us children. The culture inside the school was different then. The pedagogues used a different lexicon and explained things differently, so now there is a full culture of gestures that is gone, or understood less concretely. My own pedagogue, Alla Mikhailovna Chernova, was also born in the nineteenth century. The people in the school then received a completely different upbringing from those there now.

I spent my middle years of training under Chernova, and the last three years at the school with Lidiya Mikhailovna Tiuntina. Tiuntina had friends, male pedagogues, Boltacheyev's family. They were a couple, a wife and husband, who often came to the Academy and helped. At that time we rehearsed with men, duets, *pas de deux.* The culture of pedagogy means a lot to the student, and that relationship is very special.

I always loved turning. At the Academy we would have turning competitions, along with the other children, to see who could turn the most. We would find an empty rehearsal studio and just turn and turn. . . . I also really enjoyed pointe work. We often watched the lessons of the older girls in the rehearsal studio—even today I remember details from watching those rehearsals.

My first *pas de deux* on stage was at the end of the 3rd year there, so I was about thirteen years old. I danced *The Flames of Paris,* and the next year, in the sixth class [now known as the first course], Boris Eifman set a ballet on us called *Zhizn' na Vstretchu* (Living Forward). Tatiana Terekhova, who was graduating at the time, danced the main soloist role, and I danced her as a little girl, also a solo part.

I danced *pas de deux* beginning in the fifth class and continuing through the final year of school, and I was doing *fouettés* by the time I was age fourteen. My first solo role, however, was midway through my third year at the Academy. We had a performance just before New Year's; Chernova asked them to give me Kitri. That was very unusual at the time, because then it was expected that up to a certain age, children did not study the repertoire and should focus only on basic dances, the waltz, and so on. Kitri was considered a repertoire role, and there wasn't much precedence for a student of my age dancing a part like this. All of the other students were doing polkas and waltzes, but they allowed me to dance Kitri *en pointe* as a ballerina.

Every year at graduation I was given solo parts. At the end of my sixth year, I danced the Winter variation from Konstantin Sergeyev's *Cinderella.* It was a challenging piece with lots of jumps and turns. The next year I danced [the role of] Summer with Konstantin Zaklinsky, who was graduating. And in my final year I danced *Venice Carnavale* from *Satinella,* as well as Gulnare from the third act of *Le Corsaire.*

In my last year of studies I prepared for the International Ballet Competition at Varna. For the competition itself, I danced the

Corsaire pas de deux, The Flames of Paris solo, and Eifman's Gayané from *Luna and Karenn*.

While still in school I danced leading roles, and by the time I was in the second course [age 16] I had already danced five *pas de deux*. So, I graduated from the Academy and entered the theater as a prepared ballerina, which doesn't happen very often nowadays.

Once in the theater, I was a workaholic, but the schedule seemed light to me, I always took two classes a day. That wasn't much for me to do, I wanted more. I was prepared to dance from morning to night, whatever they would offer me. In the first two years with the Kirov I danced almost the entire solo repertoire in terms of variations under director Igor Belsky. Typically they don't like it when they give solos right away to young girls, but they did that to me, I danced the solo in Act III of *Don Quixote*—that was my very first performance in the Mariinsky Theatre. I also danced solos in *Paquita*, and *Swan Lake*. I practically didn't dance in the corps de ballet at all.

Then the directorship changed: they removed Belsky, and two years of uncertainty ensued before Vinogradov took his post. Vinogradov had been at the Maly Opera Theatre. He came to watch us, and it was at that point that I was pushed down into the corps de ballet, because the person who had wanted me only in solo parts was now gone.

Vinogradov liked tall girls, and so he first looked at those with long, thin legs. But I'm medium height, with a feminine build, and I was not favored in terms of external appearance.

One day the ballerina slated to dance in *Le Corsaire* was sick. Natalia Dudinskaya remembered seeing me dance Gulnare from Act III during my graduation performance, and insisted that I fill in for the sick dancer. Dudinskaya had overseen all of the rehearsals, so she showed me the order of the steps that morning. I wrote it down, remembered it, and danced the full-length *Le Corsaire* that same night. After that, seeing how I'd risen to the occasion, Vinogradov began slowly to give me more roles as a soloist. But I was still never satisfied, I always wanted to dance more. I filled my days off with other performing opportunities. I would often go to Estonia on Sunday night—to dance there on Monday, our one day off—and return early Tuesday morning to take class at the theater. I wanted more experience. Because then, Kurgapkina and Kolpakova were big names. It was hard to climb the ranks and get a performance—it only happened if one of them was sick or refused to dance, but that happened very rarely. It wasn't like today, when you can prepare a solo role on the side and then say to the director, "Look at me, and let me dance this." That just wasn't done back then.

I asked Irina about the first time I ever saw her dance—in a videotaped recording of *Le Corsaire* featuring Altynai Asylmuratova and Farukh Ruzimatov from the late 1980s. In it she danced one of the three Odalisque girls, pulling off a series of double and triple pirouettes, spinning like a top, and jumping as if the floor were hot. She was a powerhouse in that short variation.

I wasn't supposed to dance in the Odalisque trio. If you note in the titles of that videotape, Margarita Kulik is actually listed. At the time I was rehearsing *Don Q* in the rehearsal hall, working on a variation. The full working day had ended, but they were filming onstage. They told me, "Quick, to the dressing room. Put on stage makeup, you're dancing." Extreme. My life has always been that way.

To dance two performances in the same manner is not possible. Something new must happen, or new feelings must arise. Today the weather is one way; tomorrow it will be another. It seems to me that each partner is also different. It's a great joy and luxury to dance with the same one twice. Different eyes, different gestures, different mood—and the performance changes based on who you are dancing with and who you like. Personally I like the roles that are psycho-dramatic, where you can feel something, not just simple divertissements. Technique is a language like our words. Without language you cannot say anything. For me that is technique. . . . There are some romantic roles I enjoy[ed]. Giselle is one of them, despite the fact that she is not grounded; she is no longer human. I always wanted to give Giselle some feeling; I wanted to depict the kind of love that, when she dies, the viewer cries, so that they feel the soul dies, not just a beautiful nymph who moves, or a butterfly, but a real being.

I also saw the role of Gamzatti differently from what they wanted. You can dance this role cold and stony, crafty and sly, as if nothing is interesting to her except the fulfillment of her wishes: she wants Solor. But you can also perform it as a struggle for your love. Maybe Gamzatti really loves him or secretly loves him . . . maybe it's not a coincidence that his portrait hangs there on the wall. To me, a ballet that doesn't have a pre-history is not interesting. It's not like a movie, where you sit down, encounter part of these people's lives, and then it's over. The people lived before and after that, or not, and with ballet it is the same thing. I always tended to approach roles in that way, going beyond the span of the characters on stage, beyond the span of the curtain opening and closing.

Chistiakova graduated at the top of her class but never quite received her due at the Kirov. Nonetheless, given her vast stage experience and her early achievements, it is no surprise that she began to coach at almost the same time she began dancing:

I began to teach early in the school also, while I was still performing in the theater, so my work as a pedagogue stems from many years ago. Parents would often ask me to help with the younger children. Or other girls who needed help would ask me. Maybe because I was the best student? I don't know. I've always enjoyed teaching, explaining what is necessary in order for the movement or step to succeed. Not just copying. There are definitive geometrical and physical laws—biomechanics—that you can apply to ballet dancing. When there is a defined law, physics, a whole system is worked out. I studied these kinds of analysis and with time a basis of teaching came to me, a scientific base, why it's possible to move this way and not that. How to achieve the same result through the same steps with less energy lost, less energy output. I studied aerodynamic laws and biomechanics, and physical laws, who, how, what, and why; what incline can be taken, how bones and ligaments work for optimal results. I experimented on myself and then began to help others. If you understand what you are doing before you do it, not just do it and then break your leg, but understand it first, then you can control it.

By 2011, Chistiakova had already been coaching Lopatkina privately for six years. As in her early days at the Academy, there is still a great demand for Chistiakova's coaching wisdom inside the theater.

If I can, I help many soloists unofficially; officially I work with Lopatkina. Inside this theater, I cannot choose who I work with; the director decides that. However, because Lopatkina has a certain status in the theater, she can choose her coach. Unfortunately in the theater the director decides who works with whom, and people don't always suit each other.

I consider the pedagogue to be more than a rehearsal coach. You know the etymology of the term; a pedagogue is a "leader of children" as it is known historically. This is work that demands psychological and emotional support—you have to be able to help the person prepare for a performance so they are self-assured, not scared, and so they feel their uniqueness, because each dancer is unique. Each has a unique possibility to express emotion to the public and so that they can make an impression and create a role.

Once, I had a surprising experience. One year while I was still dancing with the company, we toured to London. I entered my dressing room and found a huge bouquet of 500 roses on my dressing table. I could not pick it up, there were so many roses, and I didn't understand why they were on my table. Maybe someone sent them to give out to the whole company after the performance, and they'd just landed in my dressing room. Then I found a letter with the roses. It read, "Two years ago I was in the city for two days, and I happened upon your performance of *Giselle*. I watched it, feeling I could not leave theater, so I looked at the schedule and saw *Giselle* would be performed the next night too, and I bought tickets and attended your second performance as well. And ever since, during these past two years, the emotional feeling I felt has never left me. The Kirov has not been in London these past two years, but when I saw that you'd be here again, I bought tickets to all of your performances." That note accompanied the gigantic bouquet of roses.

Of course we are responsible for what we convey from the stage, and the kind of feelings inside people when they leave the theater, whether they're disappointed or otherwise.

When coaching, I try to help everyone with the tiny details because dance should be intellectual. You should understand what the gesture is, what it means. Yesterday you saw a "dirty" rehearsal when we ran through the *Raymonda pas de deux* [the steps and staging]. The next rehearsals will focus on what emotions Uliana and Vanya [Kozlov] should convey, which head turns express those emotions, at what moment they turn the head, when to breathe in order to hit the musical accent, because when you teach the body that . . . because our emotions express beauty, and what you feel inside is important to express through the plasticity.

Often with dancers and actors of a high level of technical competency, they may feel a certain emotion internally, but you either cannot see it externally, or it appears differently, and the language of the body must express the feeling of our soul and emotions. Dancers must learn to express emotions with their bodies, and not grimace when they move.

The ballet life is short, it ends quickly. I don't think a dancer should go on stage if he doesn't have a concept or a vision of a role. I help them find that concept in rehearsals. Sometimes you find a few unexpected moments when a person dances a role many times and doesn't think of what it means . . . he does it a lot, but what does it mean, what can he put into it to make meaning of it? And then sometimes a little key appears that will give meaning to it.

In my mind Uliana is one of the few dancers, if not the only one, left of the Petersburg culture of dancers . . . not in terms of the quantity of technique—lift the leg as high as possible—but in terms of how to lift the leg. *How* you lift it is more important than how high it goes. And with pirouettes, whether you're doing many or a few, they must be musical. As I said before, technique is the dictionary in which all linguistic phrases are held. If you don't have the technical base, that is bad, but if you only have technique, that is also bad. It's boring. Better to go to the circus if that's the case. In the circus you can see the steps and the body without emotions or musicality, you can find the high legs there. Ballet depicts music more deeply.

I asked Chistiakova about the current trend of gymnastic-level flexibility in the lower ranks of the Mariinsky dancers in some cases at the expense of mature, developed artists.

You know, with every directorship there is a preference. "I like this dancer, so she is going to dance." That's normal. Years ago, we called it favoritism. I don't think that there are people who cannot grow and mature. You can find a tiny spark in any person and pull it out from inside. But it's another thing if that person is not interested in developing themselves, for development is hard work; it's not just about learning a new role.

"He didn't fall and he knows the order of the steps." That, in my opinion, isn't a role, that isn't really anything, I don't know what to call it, but it is not art. It is not ballet.

This tendency to promote gymnastics was not always a part of this theater. When I first began to work here, I was very troubled by it. I worried, tried to influence and explain to the administration what was going on. But usually administrators within theaters don't like people like me, because I'm insistent and independent, and I'm not here because of some special favors. These are my principles, and some people either don't like them or don't want to see them. To share your own opinion isn't always desired or appreciated.

So you can only change your relationship to the issues. The more people you can help, teaching a person to maximize his potential, those actions accomplish more than your words will. Because if the powers that be don't want to listen to you, they won't. But if they see the results of what you say, if they are capable of seeing, because not all people are—then it's possible to incite change from below, quietly.

In the theater you can only really depend on yourself. When I was dancing, there was a very formal structural process in place. You didn't just go stand at the barre in a company class next to principal dancers; that was never done. You had to ask the permission of the teacher, and he or she would agree to you taking the class, and walk you into the studio.

Under Makhar Vaziev, everyone—soloists, along with members of the corps de ballet—took the morning warm-up classes from the pedagogue of their choice. With the advent of Yuri Fateyev as head of the ballet in spring 2008, the assigned class system again returned to the theater, and each dancer must attend the class to which he or she has been assigned; only female pedagogues teach the female dancers, and only male pedagogues lead the men's classes.

Chistiakova points out that theater politics can often wreak havoc on a dancer's internal flame. "It's very easy to kill a dancer, morally speaking. If you stop giving them performances, they get out of shape, they begin to lose hope . . . it is easy to kill that desire inside someone. Ballet is an art of fanatics, dancers are dedicated people."

When asked if today's audience has changed from what it used to be, Irina concurs that shifts have happened in the common viewer's level and depth of understanding:

The language in ballet must be understood by the viewer, it is not enough to see that arms and legs move robotically. The viewer should understand the text. I think therefore that lately the type of balletomane that existed decades ago doesn't exist to the same extent. I often hear people after a performance, saying, "I didn't know who danced, everyone is the same . . ." and that's a tragedy.

The art of ballet was always meant for the elites, just like classical music. Some people prefer to listen to pop music. I love jazz, the Scorpions and Pink Floyd, Elton John. . . . I know many interesting musicians who play not only classical music. You can rearrange classical music and make a joke of it—that's a level of intellect. Unfortunately the level of intellect depends both on what the person likes and on the corresponding actions. It depends on the audience as well.

Despite her busy schedule and important role as a sought-after coach inside the Mariinsky, Chistiakova admits to missing the stage—"Not just sometimes, all the time. Honestly, I very much miss it and very much want to dance again. Classical *pas de deux* aren't very interesting for me anymore, but I could do something more modern, I adore Hans Van Manen and Jerome Robbins' work. In fact we went to Van Manen's seventy-fifth anniversary in Amsterdam, and he asked why I wasn't still dancing."

Recalling her own studio and the nonprofessionals who attended classes, Irina's response to a question about body types is enlightening. When asked if it is a good idea for those without ideal ballet bodies try to pursue the art, she answers encouragingly.

Sure. Why not? I think when you are raising a child, forbidding them or making something taboo, to tell them they are incapable is a very scary thing, it creates a complex that later expresses itself in other areas of life. Let him try, it doesn't mean he has to become professional. If you can ignite the light in someone's eyes while he talks, or let him realize his best self, help him do what he always thought was impossible . . . why not? This doesn't mean everyone must dance on the Mariinsky stage, but maybe they will become a great balletmaster who can't dance but can create some interesting ballets. You never know where it will lead.

Now it's not a secret that we have very few new balletmasters who stand on the same level as Robbins, Van Manen, Balanchine, Kylian, or Neumeier. I really liked Neumeier's *Othello*. He has very interesting creations. Uliana did his ballet called *The Lesson*. I also love Béjart and Roland Petit—these kinds of unique things. I never worked with them, but I think some of these choreographers should set new ballets intended only for her [Lopatkina], and not just give her roles that are made for others. This theater doesn't invite other balletmasters to create works for Uliana, and that is a shame.

When Chistiakova rehearses with Lopatkina, it is clear that they share a love of detailed analysis, a focus on perfecting not just the steps and the character of a certain role, but also the reason behind each movement. Irina clarifies:

Uliana understands and is interested in the same things as I am. She is very musical, intelligent and emotional. She has a unique elegance of movement.

You saw it in our rehearsal working on the lifts in *Raymonda*. There are some nuances that only a man can say to another man, such as what method should be used in a certain lift. It takes energy and strength. I can share my own approach, my own secret, how the ballerina must jump into the lift. But the way the man should lift me and the exact position of his hands, those are better explained by a male pedagogue to the male dancer, the partner. Usually I wear pointe shoes to demonstrate during rehearsal. If I do it myself, I can feel it with my own body and understand what he maybe isn't doing properly.

Given that today's generation of ballet stars has fewer "eternal" couples like Ekaterina Maximova and Vladimir Vasiliev, or Margot Fonteyn and Rudolf Nureyev, I asked Chistiakova why today everyone seems to be mixed and matched.

Constant partnerships depend on the theater politics and on the capabilities of the person's character, whether the two people suit each other or not. Vanya Kozlov looks strong behind Uliana because she is tall. It's important that both partners understand and have the same goal during rehearsals. There are many points to consider in a partnership, not only whether a step works in some performances. Sometimes a pair is not completely suited to each other physically, or maybe physically they work well together but emotionally it's not a match. So you need both. Uliana is a perfectionist, and that obviously influences who she will dance with.

I teach the dancers that when a person emits a great deal of emotion, he wears himself out. Simply being emotional is not enough onstage. Emotion has to be handled carefully; otherwise you end up with a bloodless presence. Because when you are suffering, or acting as if you are, it consumes a lot of strength. So the dancer must learn in rehearsal to display the emotions via the body, through movement, and not actually consume that much energy, or else he will wear himself out. It's a challenge.

Chistiakova has clear views on the level of dancing at the Mariinsky Theatre today, compared to that of several decades ago:

There are many differences in ballet and ballet dancers today, when compared to those of the past. Of course technique has become stronger and moved forward, but there are nuances and gestures that have been lost. It's also difficult to see the relationship between the actors or artists onstage now. It is important that before a performance, the artists discuss the ballet among themselves, so that each person doesn't simply go ahead and do what they want. You have to have that element of understanding and coordination between performers before the performance happens. Those dancing the main roles need to do this, but the corps de ballet has to as well.

This practice relates to the issue of "soul" in dancing too, because true acting onstage, playing a character, is impossible without soul. Without the element of soul, artists are simply marionettes. The famous "Russian soul" is an element that has always been acknowledged in our art form, and the soul has to be implemented; you take everything from the music and dramatically express the music itself, but you have to have your own conception of it.

This soul, this emotion, whether it is present or not in the artist depends on their level of intellect; it depends on whether the dancer thinks about what he's doing and how he can put soul into it. But it also depends on the dancer's individual strengths; some people have more or less "soul" to offer. It is hard work to develop that emotional, soulful element in dance, and you need to have an individual approach; it's an issue of serious concern in a theater of this size. In a big company, you have to cultivate the artists, because they're the next generation.

Another issue is that when I graduated, the dancers of that era graduated fully prepared as ballet artists. We were further developed in the theater, but we did not need to be taught. Today the dancers enter the theater and still need to be taught. This is one major difference.

Chistiakova believes that the shift in training and the supposed lower level of preparation of today's graduates, as she sees it, pose a challenge to the Vaganova heritage itself:

There is a risk of losing the Vaganova style because unfortunately what Vaganova taught, I don't see it in the pupils today. They consider her theory old and outdated, that ballet must move forward. But move forward to what? That is the question that has to be asked. Higher legs do not mean we're moving forward. More *fouettés* also doesn't indicate progress, per se. The form must be preserved because otherwise . . .

I graduated in 1975, and performed more than 100 *fouettés* at that time, so it isn't as if this is new. High legs can be too high. In *Giselle* or *The Sleeping Beauty*, splits are not the aesthetic of those ballets. If you are dancing Forsythe or Kylian, something modern or jazzy, then please, be my guest, lift the legs as much as you want. But in Vaganova the issue is how you lift the leg and how much you move the torso and where you position the arms in accordance with the leg height. It is a physiological issue and the splits are not beautiful. Earlier it was considered improper to display legs at the heights we often see today. But ballet, the word "ballet" comes from the words "aesthetic" and "beauty." Another example, it used to be considered a sign of intimacy to display the inner part of your elbow. And that is how the pose of *allongé* developed.

All gestures have meaning. If you open the wrists, that expresses something else. There are classical gestures and other gestures, and based on the way the gestures are done, the body, wrists, fingers, and head, the gesture can shift its meaning from adequate to amazing. Unfortunately now practically all gestures have disappeared from ballet's lexicon.

So, can you combine these new aesthetics, higher legs and so on, with Vaganova style? No, because the legs must be lifted in a certain way, the poses must be balanced, in order to adhere to Vaganova's style. There are defined moments in ballet when the torso accompanies the legs, and the arms express the emotion. Now you increasingly see dancers who have the legs working along with the torso all the time; or else everything working independently, uncoordinated, and that's not the way it should be. The foundation, the basics must always be present, but there should never be just one version of this coordination, never just a monotonous movement.

Chistiakova's views are echoed by the ballerina she coaches, Uliana Lopatkina.

The Quintessential Petersburg Ballerina: Uliana Lopatkina

Uliana Lopatkina is known in Petersburg circles for her perfectionism, professionalism, pristine classicism, and adherence to the "Vaganova style" that has characterized the Petersburg ballet for decades. A student of Natalia Dudinskaya, who was one of Vaganova's closest friends and prize pupils, Lopatkina also worked extensively with Kurgapkina and has thus been the recipient of a direct line of training that leads straight to Agrippina Yakovlevna. As the carrier of such a heritage, Lopatkina is acknowledged and respected among colleagues, peers, and viewers for her taste, style, and elegance. Critic Vadim Gaevsky writes of Lopatkina in his book, *Dom Petipa* (House of Petipa), describing her

> sharpness of movement and pose, [and] the unexpected impact of big, decisive *battements*. This rare composition of mysterious uncertainty in all facets of the soul, and this clear phrasing was almost calligraphy, almost an impeccable drawing. But within this whole—the laws of the Balanchine school and that spaciousness, that intriguing and even harmonious inconsistency of internal and external properties which express the talents of newcomers—the strict academic exercises were especially evident.[25]

He calls her as well a "symphonic ballerina," one born of the symphonic ballet, the Balanchine ballet, where "her unique sense of poses are revealed; and that something that was lost, that something absent even in the dancers of the new Petersburg school was revived, and even blossomed in front of our eyes. We refer to the unusual ... talent of classical adagio, the gift of slow tempi, of cantilena. In Lopatkina this sincere gift is not cultivated, but inborn." Further:

> ... The taste of the epoch, its unchanging rhythm, the new and, to a significant degree urban sense of beauty, and at last, a completely new impression of ideal femininity in ballet theater—the Vaganova classes spurred all of this, giving it an unheard-of energy, a swiftness

and head-turning virtuosity. . . ."The fire of life," as Tolstoy wrote, describing Kitty. Unsurprisingly, this ballerina also danced Kitty in *Anna Karenina* for the Mariinsky Ballet. It is a rare case of an almost ideal concurrence of the dancer and the role . . .

Put more simply, hers is a multifaceted talent, rich with the trait of individuality. And this is the truth. Lopatkina is talented beyond typical measures.[26]

Surprisingly, despite being trained at the Vaganova Academy by Dudinskaya, who has been described as "bubbling champagne on stage," Lopatkina is not a soubrette, not a bravura dancer in the old sense of the shorter, jumping-and-turning ballerinas of old. Her long, exquisite lines and tall stature make her an ideal adagio ballerina, and she has cultivated this aspect of her art to perfection. Even Gaevsky wrote:

Urbanist dancers in the virtuosic allegro of Vaganova imitated Dudinskaya, one of Vaganova's best students, a direct continuation of her pedagogical method. Lopatkina is a student of Dudinskaya and also one of her best. Yet she was able to distance herself from [imitating] her mentor, the delicate girl had an independent and strong character. That is why Lopatkina's adagio does not render antiquity, for it is one of more modern style. The dancer expands it into all conceivable breadth and leads it on such a scale of unhurried and smooth tempi. But suddenly she will make a fascinatingly sharp half-turn, and we understand how much impetuosity, zeal and even passion is concealed in this fluid stream of melodious lines.[27]

Perhaps most succinctly, "All of Lopatkina's dancing beauty, from the cold beauty of her lines and poses, to the expression of the beauty of classical tragedy, are the distant, undying foundation of the Petersburg school."[28]

Catching Lopatkina in a free moment is difficult for even the most professional and well-connected journalist. She rarely grants interviews and retains a level of privacy that is understood and respected by those in the Petersburg theater world. As the single purest representative of true Vaganova style in the Mariinsky Ballet today, her views on her art and Vaganova's style carry great weight.

Left: Irina Chistiakova as Giselle, a role that she excelled in according to witnesses, but rarely danced. Photo: Yulia Larionova.

Below: Uliana Lopatkina as the white swan Odette, in *Swan Lake*. Never distorting the lines, Lopatkina's pure technique exemplifies the Vaganova method especially in this role. Photo: Natalia Razina.

Uliana Lopatkina in *Giselle*. Photo: Natalia Razina.

Uliana Lopatkina as Raymonda with Danila Korsuntsev as Jean de Brienne, in the ballet *Raymonda*. The full-length version is performed at the Mariinsky but rarely done in other ballet companies around the world. Photo: Natalia Razina.

She agreed to speak briefly during a short post-rehearsal break during the company's single day off one summer month.[29] Without makeup, Lopatkina's flawless complexion serves as a background to amber eyes, a short crop of ginger hair, pixie style, a soft, gentle voice, and sinewy limbs accentuated by her dance attire. Self-deprecating in other interviews, she has called herself unattractive, but nothing could be further from the truth. If anything, this humble ballerina holds within her a strange dichotomy: meekness, sky-high standards, and a reluctant acceptance of the icon she has become. This combination of traits produces a grounded professional who is thoughtful, serious, and highly analytical in all she says and does. She speaks first about what the Vaganova style is, as she understands it:

> The Vaganova style is defined by a harmonious composition of all poses, the movement of the head, arms, and legs. It is what distinguishes the art of ballet from sports. The system she developed gives you a clear idea about how, practically speaking, to achieve beauty in motion. What for me is very important is that it is a very understandable format of the work of the body where all of the laws of biomechanics are considered. You can use this system in the modern system of classical ballet as well. Today's movements, which are distinguished from the former period and style of classical ballet, have more amplitude, height, and width, and even with these shifts, the foundations of classical ballet, the method of Vaganova, remains the same. Thus I consider it to be quite universal.
>
> More concretely, I can say that Vaganova developed special requirements for the positions of the arms and torso with regard to how they interact with each other; for example, she lifted the elbows, lowered the shoulders, and on the basis of these biomechanical shifts, the spectator receives a sense of free and strong movement. There is no sense of impairment of the body, the lines are not shortened and sharpened, but lengthened; physically it is similar to what in music is called *legato*. There is a very strong connection between the Vaganova system and the specific traits of the Mariinsky Ballet today.

The close relationship between Dudinskaya, who was Lopatkina's main teacher when she graduated from the Vaganova Academy, and

Agrippina Yakovlevna herself has been noted by many Russian writers. Kremshevskaya noted how Dudinskaya adopted Vaganova's method with surprising exactness, persistence, and love. And how Vaganova, in turn, very stern toward work, incited the full devotion and faith of her students in her method.[30] Dudinskaya herself declared that Vaganova was the "single pedagogue who not only taught, but was also able to seize upon and reveal the inexhaustible possibilities of classical dance."[31] Lopatkina mentions the link between the two pedagogues:

> Both Dudinskaya and Kurgapkina spoke to me about Vaganova, and their tales unify one basic idea about Vaganova. Agrippina Yakovlevna was very strict in rehearsals; she even displayed brutality—not rigidity, but cruelty—even if you were her favorite student. However, her demands were very understandable and clear. She loved her students and didn't allow them to become lazy.

At the mention of the shifting aesthetics in ballet today, Lopatkina is very frank and direct in her response. She doesn't hesitate to point out that the Vaganova style can be preserved even while adopting new "trends" in dance, but that it must be done with extreme care:

> The tendency of modern classical ballet to change the measure of degree of the pose, the approach toward what is artistic gymnastics, it's my opinion that the Vaganova system saves classical ballet from entering into sports, if you understand her system correctly. What is "correctly"? I can explain: no matter how high you lift the leg, each position must be a harmonious composition that incorporates the diagonals of the legs, arms, and the pose of the head. So you have to look very carefully at how high to lift the leg. The requirements of beauty must be harmoniously combined together; if you pay specific attention to the beauty of line, then classical ballet remains ballet even under the changes in the degrees of a position. The line must be logical.
>
> For example, earlier they lifted the leg here [she lifts her right leg to the side in *à la seconde* 95 degrees from the floor, displaying a perfectly turned out and pointed foot]. Now they lift it here [she demonstrates 160 degrees]. That is also high, no? The diagonal is here, in *écarté* [she gestures to the line that begins with the toes of her

lifted leg]. I don't lift the leg to my shoulder [she demonstrates 180 degrees] because then the pose is completely ruined. If the leg remains on the diagonal [at around 160 degrees], then the opposing arm must be lowered [she places her left arm in a low *demi-seconde* pose that matches the angle of the line begun with the toes of her lifted right leg], and the torso is also shifted over, accordingly. You cannot have the leg here [180 degrees] and then dip the torso and lower the arm—that isn't *écarté* anymore.

Another example: if dancers lift *attitude derrière* very high [she lifts one leg behind her, bending her torso forward slightly, until her legs form a 180-degree line in *attitude penché*], then you can't lift the spine. A logical line must be drawn from one point on the body to the next. This is not an issue of returning to the old poses of the past but of perfecting the new ones. It is like a new level of harmony. Vaganova's system allows you to understand where that harmony lies and find the new framework of classical ballet. The system of Vaganova cultivates the logical implementation of poses.

Based on Lopatkina's demonstrations, it is clear that her approach to leg and arm height is based on the beauty and harmony that she alludes to. It is not a question of hitting a certain number of degrees in a pose or displaying the extent of personal flexibility: instead, the lines of the body are always considered; they must be balanced at all times.

Given Lopatkina's work with some of the most famous names in St. Petersburg ballet, her views on the role of the pedagogue in the life of a ballerina are interesting. She explains:

The role of pedagogue? Maybe you can compare it to [the trainer in] sports or artistic gymnastics. In addition to the training and psychological help and guidance that the pedagogue offers to the dancer, the pedagogue-*répétiteur* has a very important role, comparable to the *regisseur*, or stage director in a dramatic theater. They [pedagogues] are *regisseurs* of the *plastique* of a concrete individual, a concrete ballerina; directors of the emotions which must be visible in the dancer's *plastique*. Practically speaking, I can say that they play a fundamental role in the life of a ballerina, alongside her strength of will, diligence, intelligence, and her physical traits. Without a pedagogue, realizing these capabilities is many times

Uliana Lopatkina as "The Dying Swan," which many consider her signature role. Photo: Natalia Razina.

more difficult, and often the results that are achieved in union with the pedagogue-rehearsal coach cannot be achieved otherwise. That is, if the union functions well, of course.

I can add that I'm a happy ballerina because during one of the most difficult times of my life, after the birth of my child, I met Irina Chistiakova and asked her to help me strengthen the training which I very much needed in order to get back into shape after pregnancy. It wasn't enough for me to simply have rehearsals as before. She adopted a serious workload with me, and thanks to our work together I have eliminated some health problems that appeared during the very difficult physical work of these years. I found in her a like-minded person, an ally in the understanding of creative, artistic work. In her various roles she considers herself a pedagogue-*répétiteur*, psychologist, and sports trainer. She helps determine what the level of workload will be and how to construct classes so as not to overload you, but also not to let you become too lazy.

In mentioning the pedagogue aiding the ballerina with the element of emotion, Lopatkina clarifies that this is part of every dancer's responsibility as a professional artist:

Can a person learn the element of dramatism in ballet? As a dancer you must learn it. Ballet is theater; it is not a competition and it is not a sport. It is a theatrical art. So you need to cultivate not just dancers, but actors. Ballet is also not just dance in cafés, with the goal of pleasing the viewers who sit at a table; it's not just dance as movement; it carries a much more artistic content. It isn't called an *art* for no reason. There must be an element of soul given to ballet throughout one's life. And you have to have the technique of acting in ballet in order to do this.

Curious about how this icon of an art that harks back to the tsarist period gravitated to ballet, I inquired about her impetus to study it:

I began to dance because I loved to move to music as a small child. My mother decided to develop this desire and capability, first with general dancing and then with ballet. And life just followed from there. I never had concrete thoughts of becoming a ballerina. As a child I was obedient and quiet. At five years old they sent me to buy groceries, and I went alone. But I could never have dreamed of becoming a ballerina; it never entered my head to cultivate such a dream.

Lopatkina's parting words attest to a recognition of the rapid progress in our world, and the potential threat it poses to this very special art form over time:

One hundred years from now I would like to see the preservation of the beauty of movement in ballet, and the presence of the element of soul, that the feelings and emotions that the dancers emit on stage are also felt by the audience. I also hope that with our flight forward in civilization and technical progress, the advent of computer games and animation, that this art will still be needed by people 100 years from now. That the living body, the living movements, the living soul, the nerves, the warmth that comes from a live dancer will still be appreciated and necessary.

A Cultural Catastrophe

Sergei Vikulov, former Kirov ballet star who graduated in 1956 and performed until 1988, a decorated Honored Artist of the RSFSR, and People's Artist of both the RSFSR and USSR, is now a renowned pedagogue in his own right. Since 1998 he has worked inside the Mariinsky as coach and *répétiteur*, and he sees the issue of Vaganova's traditions from a much broader perspective. With flyaway gray hair and vibrant gestures, Vikulov enthusiastically explains his point of view.[32]

Agrippina Yakovlevna Vaganova came from the Silver Age, a time of great composers and choreographers and artists. Mikhail Fokine's "The Russian Seasons" toured England and America back then. Vaganova united everything; she synthesized the best from the French and Italian and Russian schools of the time, and created a unique methodology of ballet teaching. Hers is a deep poetry of movement, a philosophy and aesthetic, all encompassed in one

Sergey Vikulov as Siegfried in *Swan Lake*, 1964. He says Vaganova approached her training system "not from the point of view of training, but from the point of view of art." Vikulov now coaches male dancers inside the Mariinsky Theatre. Photo: Borisov.

"school," one method of training. She approached it, however, not from the point of view of training, but from the point of view of art, of Petipa and Fokine, of great artists.

She was able to find her position in the world at that time, but now, today, the aesthetic is gone. The idea of "art" as we know it is no longer found in life, but in death. Woman has ceased being an object of art, inspired by God and inspiring to man; women used to be praised for their beauty—sculptures, paintings, musical compositions were created in ode to women. They are no longer objects of art; they now are considered the same as men—they dress like men, talk like men, work like men—even in ballet, they most often perform the same movements as men. They are male "equals" today. The great aesthetic in which lies the idea of female beauty—Petipa used this as well—that philosophy, that approach to art and to life is gone.

We are in the midst of a deep cultural catastrophe, on a global scale. Not in the execution of art—people can produce art, or what is considered art today—but in the creation of it. The philosophy of aesthetics has changed, all across the world. We have talented people now, but there is a festering illness. The number of *cabrioles* is not important, rather what they are about, why are they performed?

The last great ballet created on the Mariinsky Theatre was Grigorovich's *The Legend of Love* [1961]. If you consider how long ago it was created, that speaks to the death of true cultural richness, of cultural innovation. My opinion is unlikely to be heard because the selection of movements used nowadays . . . the entire world is afraid of revealing their stupidity. You see a square canvas painted entirely black, and it sells for millions of dollars. Why? Where is the art? Because, you see, if you pay for it, it means you understand the depth of this "art." It's like the Emperor's New Clothes—no one can say the king is naked, no one is allowed to speak the truth, and this applies to art everywhere in the world now. Now there are good interpreters, but no more great ideas, no more innovation. And if there are talented artists, they aren't given a road or area in which to cultivate their talents, because today art is most of all politics—not the politics you read of in the newspapers, but the politics of aesthetics, and in an eternal sense of the world. Morality, love, these are all in a state of global deep depression. The search now is to find a black cat in a dark room—of course you can do it, but you need to lighten the room first.

Coincidentally, decades ago Mikhail Fokine recorded similar observations in an article published in the emigré newspaper, *Novoe Russkoe Slovo* (New Russian Word) in 1935:

If I compare my dreams with what I see on the contemporary stage, then I come to a sad conclusion: despite all of the noise about modernization, about external achievements, about the relationship to the breath of the new life and so on and so forth, today's ballet repeats all the mistakes of the old classical ballet, adding to it the biggest mistake of all—a loss of sincerity and a waste of the sensation of truth.

People ask me: what are the mistakes of classical ballet that modern is repeating? How is it possible, how did ballet depart from the old?

Nothing has departed!

They still dance *en pointe* and perform a French *pas de bourrée* in the scene of a Russian village wedding, at the myth of Prometheus. . . . Just as in the old ballet there was an absence of true gestures, style of movement, so today all is replaced once and for all with a fabricated form of dance.

In the old ballet this was the form of the refined elegance of the French-Italian school.

Now this image of grotesque acrobatic style rejects the beauty of a normal, healthy body. Grotesque, eccentric . . . maybe there is a place for it; it may all be fine in its place, but when you repeat it . . . using it in all cases, then it is the same mistake that occurred in the old ballet.[33]

The aesthetics of the 1920s and 1930s seemed to Fokine grotesque at times. Similarly, the aesthetics of today's high legs and split *ecartés* seem grotesque to those who trained under Vaganova just decades ago.

Vikulov is not alone in his sentiments. In 1978, a similar view was expressed by Vera Kostrovitskaya:

You see more rarely that artistic coordination of movements for which Agrippina Yakovlevna so fiercely fought. The young artists, having finished school, in the best case, are coached to perform . . . modern tricks, but are not masters of the complex knowledge and manner in full volume. Moreover, we are now hearing the claim that "The Vaganova method is old!"

In my view it is more important to recall the details of Vaganova's profession—not just the artistic galas, but the daily work in cultivating future ballet artists. With great disappointment you see now that even the Leningrad Choreographic School . . . is beginning to move away from the concealed difficulties in this method; they are tempted by easier methods of teaching. As a result, instead of comprehensive training, the participants acquire weak professional preparation. . . . There is none of the required attention to the work of the torso and hands. Static, near immobility leads the dancer. . . . The partial strictness in the position of the wrists has been lost, as has the freedom of shoulder movement which Vaganova achieved.

. . . The orientation of our pedagogues to the mediocre level of foreign guest performers, in my deep conviction, is not at all justified. Think for yourself: doesn't it prove to be a paradox that foreign ballet dancers envy the Russian ballet school, its traditions and methods? If you imagine the slightest possibility of coming to the Soviet Union to study our method of teaching classical dance, to adopt it . . . And at this time we don't value the method; we are prepared to announce it as old and unnecessary; we prefer to "coach" the students in pursuit of cheap public success, of showy "window dressing," not worrying that in the process we're losing the most valuable thing: the achievements of our own Soviet school of dance.

From time to time innovators appear on the pedagogical horizon, offering to bring acrobatics or some sort of "speedy" methods for developing the musculature of the legs in classical training. Most often, these promising "stretches" lead to professional injury. . . . The position of the Russian, and in part the Leningrad School of Classical Dance has become serious. With sadness you look at the youths graduating each year: they're taught to turn, but are helpless at the most important element: dance itself.[34]

Kostrovitskaya's argument acknowledges a key point: no matter what the internal disagreements regarding the status of the Russian system, history has proven Vaganova's training system invaluable. Her School still produces some of the world's greatest dancers, dancers who are frequently the envy of those in America or Europe, individuals who become great ballerinas or great male dancers and remain unparalleled the world over in their unique style, expressiveness, and clean technique. Kostrovitskaya complained of a perceived loss of the true Vaganova method, the Russian style of ballet dancing, over twenty years ago, just as today's pedagogues voice similar concerns. But to accept these critiques as a sign of a failed system would be to miss the broader view. Such appraisals come from a strict, internal perspective, one of the struggle for perfection within a decades-old system that remains a measurement of quality throughout the ballet world. Indeed, to observe the classes at the Vaganova Academy today, or to see the lines of the Mariinsky corps de ballet alongside Lopatkina on stage in *Swan Lake* today, is to eliminate nearly all of the dissenting pedagogues' concerns. Clearly, among today's Vaganova students, and inherent in select ballerinas such as Lopatkina, a great deal of this glorious legacy remains and even flourishes.

Konstantin Shatilov expressed the urgency of preserving this tradition before his death in 2003:

We must save the classical heritage. The great classical productions remain only in Russia and the surrounding countries. I don't understand why the theater is always remaking Petipa. They took masterpieces—*The Sleeping Beauty, The Nutcracker, La Bayadère*—and spoiled these ballets. Balletmasters of the Soviet epoch continued to develop a line assembled in pre-revolutionary times. Fyodor Vasilievich Lopukhov related to Lev Ivanov and Marius Petipa very protectively. . . . But now producers redo the old productions, breaking their style. I don't speak against innovation: set the unknown ballets of Petipa, take some new interesting theme. But why ruin the former repertoire? And then they say that Vaganova's method is old, the classical repertoire is old. It is the same as saying the music of Bach, Mozart, and Beethoven has outlived its century and become obsolete.[35]

More hopeful voices contradict these morose thoughts. In his own published commentary, Konstantin Sergeyev reinforces Vaganova's belief in living, growing, developing art, and quotes her diary, pointing out that Vaganova did not consider the classics to be museum pieces:

[Vaganova wrote:] "If the music, the poetry of great art remains eternal, then with time another requirement appears in stage art, the requirements of the age. The technique of art changes. The viewer seeks more spirituality, more realism, [and] that is especially noticeable in ballet. The dancer seeks new means of execution. The producer of this or that production also changes, goes forward, is infected with the spirit of the new epoch. This happened also in ballet with *Swan Lake*."

We must remember her covenant: "everything in life is growing, moving forward, blooming. Therefore I recommend keeping in touch with life and art."[36]

Based on Vaganova's own intentions, moving forward is necessary in order to infuse the art of ballet with ever-fresh ideas and concepts. Agrippina Yakovlevna would hardly have supported the evolution of ballet into other forms of dance if it meant the eventual disappearance of the foundation she worked so hard to lay, the classical exercise and methodology. Nonetheless, her own textbook points out that Vaganova

by no means regarded her instructional system as immutable or fixed once and for all. Guided by her vast experience, Vaganova's pupils are enriching and amending this instructional system in their creative practice. Thus, a number of ballet classes now give successful exercises on the high, not the low, half-toes (*demi-pointe*). In the last few years the [Russian] expansion of cultural ties has created the possibility of the international exchange of creative experience in the field of choreographic instruction, as in other fields. The people concerned with Soviet ballet have not failed to notice the achievements of foreign dancers in the area of ballet technique, particularly in *tours* and virtuoso beats. . . . Perfecting the methodology of teaching ballet, enriching the lexicon and emotional expressiveness of movements, the Soviet instructors, followers of Vaganova, are striving to make their choreographic school correspond to the current level of Soviet balletic art, augmenting its glory.[37]

Today in the post-Soviet era, the Vaganova Academy continues that tradition of incorporating external foreign influences when appropriate, but adhering to the system codified by Agrippina Vaganova.

Altynai Asylmuratova—
Artistic Director, Vaganova Academy

The Vaganova School of Russian Ballet on Rossi Street in St. Petersburg continues to function today just as it did over 200 years ago. Each June, hundreds of students along with their parents line up outside the famous pale yellow building for the initial entrance selection process. The prestige of a diploma from the Vaganova Academy carries with it more than just glamour: it ensures employment in one of the country's theaters, if not the Mariinsky or Bolshoi, then the Mikhailovsky, Stanislavsky, or one of many numerous other venues. A dancer hired by the Mariinsky or Bolshoi, barring any debilitating injury, has a chance at stardom and, if they work the requisite twenty years, a guaranteed pension by age thirty-seven or thirty-eight. In sum, it is a career track that is still partially state sponsored, and more stable than many other professions in Russia.

Applicants who pass the first round of auditions are asked to return for a second round that includes a medical evaluation in which experts measure the children's bones, height, and weight against a set of growth estimates. Flexibility, insteps, and external appearance are also taken into account. Those selected begin the nine-year course of study in September, and must pass through two rounds of school eliminations, generally after the third and fifth years of study. After the seventh year of study, the weaker students are given diplomas of "general education" and dismissed with the option of applying for the final two years and receiving the baccalaureate diploma, the degree granted to all who complete the nine-year course. There is now also an optional track to receive a master's degree, but typically graduates leave to work in theaters for at least ten years before returning to obtain it.

The nine-year course of study at the Academy includes academic subjects, mandatory lessons in a musical instrument, dance history, acting lessons, character dance and *pas de deux*, among others.

The Academy's current artistic director, former Kirov ballerina

As the director of the Vaganova Academy, Altynai Asylmuratova strives to guard Vaganova's system of teaching. "From the first class through to graduation, in the end [this training system] results in the crowning accomplishment of perfect execution." Here she is shown as Medora in *Le Corsaire* during her dancing years. Photo: Yulia Larionova.

Asylmuratova as Medora in *Le Corsaire*. Photo: Natalia Razina.

Altynai Asylmuratova, assumed her post in 2001 after a brilliant stage career in which she was often paired with Farukh Ruzimatov both at home and on foreign tours.

As director of the school, Asylmuratova must look after its standards. She aids in the student selection process each year and handles various administrative duties, even overseeing graduation rehearsals and annual year-end examinations.

Formerly a leading ballerina in the Kirov Theatre, Asylmuratova now passes on her knowledge to students at the Vaganova Academy. Photo: Stanislav Belyaevsky.

Asylmuratova's responsibilities include preparing the Academy's students for their annual performances. Photo: Stanislav Belyaevsky.

When she began her post, Asylmuratova wrote an essay for the Vaganova Academy's publication, *Vestnik*, that read in part:

Now we need to return to what for some reason seems lost. Only then can we move forward. I worked abroad a lot and know both the values and deficiencies of various schools. I do not suggest we change our method to, let's say, the French method, which has clean leg work but does not have our arms and our torso coordination. We must soberly evaluate our own results, we must see our weaknesses and use others' achievements.[38]

Asylmuratova's early intent to continuously reevaluate the Academy's offerings is a promise to herself and to the school, and she has kept it. Deep in the halls of the Academy, her word, her view, and her vision speak for years of tradition as she now upholds the legacy of Agrippina Vaganova's life and work.

A brief visit into her roomy office on the fourth floor of the Academy provides the opportunity to discuss how the directorship approaches the Vaganova method, and how it is preserved today in the classrooms of this famous building. A desk littered with videotapes and DVDs, drafts of schedules, and other documents attests to the constant business of her position. In a break between graduation rehearsals and auditions for next year's students, Asylmuratova explains Vaganova training as the ideal foundation for any classical dancer.

This system prepares you to dance any classical variation or ballet. Everything is included in its lessons. Vaganova actually systematized her method; she is considered the first professor who, roughly speaking, "scientifically" developed a system for teaching children [ballet]. For each year of study there is a stronger workload that drives the students' development. From the first class through to graduation, in the end it results in the crowning accomplishment of perfect execution.

But Vaganova's legacy goes beyond the perfect execution of steps. Might changes in time and fashion affect or alter the style itself? Asylmuratova answers definitively:

No, in general, we can say that everything remains as it was. Some elements perhaps a bit more or a bit less, depending, but the essence of the Vaganova style remains. To say that nothing changes at all would not be true. Some elements have left, and some have appeared. That doesn't mean the system itself is imperfect, but that the given period of time in question demands it—because you also understand, in each era there are different requirements, and we adapt, without eliminating tradition.

Now we have begun to develop modern dance more; we have begun to value and to use physical traits like greater leg height and flexibility (*bolshoi shag*) more. These things are necessary, but it is very important not to lose the main essence of ballet, because in the end, ballet is not a sport, it is an art. Just as sports include some elements of ballet, so some elements of sport enter into ballet. But ballet is an art and we must not lose the essence: the richness, the spirituality, the taste, the style, these things should not be lost due only to some circus steps or movements.

The style will not change. It is hard to explain, but in our profession the tradition passes from hand to hand, from foot to foot, no matter how much time elapses. Vaganova taught her students, and her students in turn taught other students, and so on. In this manner the information will be passed down from generation to generation. It goes practically by the book, even her textbook itself says you cannot fully master the style and method of Agrippina Yakovlevna, because ballet is a live art, and each pedagogue is like a sculptor of each individual, and they must explain the nuances.

This apparently flexible approach to the living art of ballet is what prevents the Academy from falling into stagnation and dogma, and allows it to maintain a competitive place on the world stage, upholding classical traditions while adapting to the changing times. Asylmuratova points out that the school's pedagogues pass through a strict selection process that ensures Vaganova's legacy is upheld, and only the best pedagogues are allowed to teach:

> What is important for our future pedagogues as well is that we don't accept just any person who danced at one time or who enjoys ballet into the Pedagogical Faculty here at the school. They must all have a diploma from either the Academy or from a specific list of qualified institutions, and they also must have worked at least ten years in a state or official government opera-and-ballet theater. These are people who have practice and experience, not just anyone. So as long as this system exists, her method will remain alive.

This tight system of passing the proverbial torch onto future generations is what ensures the continuation and preservation of the Vaganova method over time and sets it apart from other schools where the requirements are less rigid. By the same token, the Academy's flexibility and avoidance of dogma is in fact a built-in component of the preservation process. The stability of the system, its reliance on the same academic plan based on Vaganova's methods, does not render it archaic or stale. Instead, processes are in place to constantly reevaluate what the school has to offer:

We look at the program every few years, which steps or movements are working, which ones are moving forward—or on the other hand, moving backward—based on their quality, and we act accordingly. But in principle the system remains as it was set, because it is a proven, tested system that is nearly 100 years old, and there is no reason to reinvent the bicycle.

Of course some of the requirements change with time. In one period we really focused on the cleanliness of the footwork, that is, their positions. But that doesn't mean we changed the method itself, because the method has everything; it doesn't mean, for example, that fifth position was eliminated. No, it still remains.

Each year our Methodology Department and our professors, and docents, and so on, these high-level professional people and professors, they look at what we have, evaluate what we need more of, what we need to pay more attention to. Each year it is a living system, not a dry one. They look at what we need to pay more attention to.

I ask if the Methodology Department remains intact and fully functional, as it was decades ago. Asylmuratova replies:

The Methodology Department has always existed, whether you refer to it as such or not, but our School, in our city—mostly in our School—we try to maximally preserve the best of what we have. For example, we try to preserve in the School what is best from the [Mariinsky] Theatre's repertoire, some dance numbers and fragments from ballets that are not performed at the theater frequently. We preserve them here in the School so that something remains, because later on they will be needed again, and then it will be easier to revive them. Such preservation also relates to our legacy.

That this system of checks and balances acts as an internal reinforcement of the method itself speaks further to the strength of tradition within the Academy. What other ballet school in the world has this rich history, this much knowledge, and a formal means of reevaluating it year after year? Asylmuratova's comments acknowledge the necessity of adapting with the times, preserving the past while moving forward, and considering modern trends in movement in order to stay current. In fact this is precisely what Vaganova herself wanted: despite her conservative approach to the art of classical ballet, Agrippina Yakovlevna held a decidedly open-minded, analytical approach to technique. But there is one key to the Vaganova system, and that, Asylmuratova explains, is the pedagogue-coach. Asylmuratova concurs with her predecessors that pedagogues play a fundamental, irreplaceable role in the preparation of a dancer from the very start.

> The most important thing at the School is the pedagogue. Everything depends on the quality of the pedagogues, the specialist pedagogues, because what they offer is not just knowledge of the theory of our profession, and not just the ability to explain to the students. The pedagogue must also be a psychologist; (s)he must be able to excite the students, and find the key to each individual personality, because people are different; there are capable but lazy students; there are less lazy but very hard-working students; there are average students, all different kinds of students. For the pedagogue, each student is a child, and each child must be loved. The pedagogue is concerned with the best results, not just throwing information out, because achieving a professional level in their students is considered prestigious for them as well.
>
> Of course all of us who studied here, we all remember and continue to love our pedagogues dearly all of our lives.

Asylmuratova wrote of the lack of middle-aged or younger pedagogues when she first assumed her post. Now she points out that age itself is not in fact always a reliable indicator of what a pedagogue has to offer.

> Age is a very loose concept. Because you can be old at age forty, or at eighty be very young and active. Each person has his or her own internal clock. Insofar as a person is interested and can give energy to interest the students, that is how young they are.
>
> If you speak about the replacement of generations, then in these [recent] years, there have been many pedagogues of various ages, middle-aged, and older ones and younger ones, and some of them we have to part with because it doesn't work out, and others we keep and develop further. It's the way the process is, and it must

be this way. It's good that we have the older generation of masters from whom we can learn, and who can share their experience with us.

Asylmuratova also acknowledges the difference between Russian dancers of the past and those on stage today, but points out that we cannot—and most likely should not—value one over the other. In contradiction to the pedagogues who bemoan a lack of emotion in modern ballet choreography or even in classical performances by today's generation of dancers, Asylmuratova is philosophical, even welcoming, about the evolution of aesthetics—and incorporating them into the Vaganova style. She continues:

> Of course, in some things they differ. Now we have stricter requirements about physical appearance. Because if you look at the 1940s and 1950s, you can go to the [Vaganova Academy] museum and look at photographs, and there were fantastic dancers then, but it is unlikely that they would become leading dancers today, because they were short and plump. Now the demands are completely different; everyone has to be thin and long. The traits are completely different today. However, it wouldn't be correct to say, I cannot say that they danced *worse*, for example. No. There were some elements that were more emotional then; the requirements were different. There were lots of ballets with stories, and we know that some of the artists fulfilling this or that role, they were truly *artists* of ballet, not just executors of movement, not just performers of subject-less technical movement. Then it was full, rich, spiritual dancing which is what Russian ballet has always been distinguished by—its emotionality and soulful richness.
>
> Today there are a lot of modern and neoclassical productions appearing in the repertoire which also demand some sort of emotional richness, but not that kind. And now there is a cleaner execution. But to say it was worse before, no.
>
> Each period has its own characteristics. For example, I still watch films with [Galina] Ulanova with great pleasure. And it completely doesn't bother me that her legs are not by her ears. I just enjoy it and I relax. It is all understandable, and touching. It seems to me that that is true art.

Vaganova Academy student. Photo: Stanislav Belyaevsky.

Asylmuratova's adamancy about the spiritual side of dance underlines the fact that technical execution alone is not the focus at the Vaganova Academy. Coming from a Vaganova-trained, former Kirov ballerina such as Asylmuratova, the comment speaks volumes. As Alla Osipenko points out, not a single pedagogue today can replicate the genius of Agrippina Vaganova: "She was the brilliant pedagogue." It seems logical, then, that as the official voice of the Vaganova Academy, Asylmuratova cannot possibly address all of the criticisms that pedagogues or parents may hold toward the institution she now directs. But as the guardian of this centuries-old tradition, she is the one now positioned to make the decisions. Whatever changes she may implement, that the Vaganova Academy holds a place close to her heart is also clear in her final statement before we part ways:

Long after I'm gone, I hope this Academy still exists. I hope that everything remains as it is, because it is a holy place. I hope that after many years the directors remain as wise as they were 271 years ago until now, because our school came into existence under the tsars who carefully preserved it, and under the Soviet government who also very much valued and preserved it, and understood the meaning of this institution. I hope the School remains in its place. I would hope also that this amazing spirit and the endless love for the profession will always be preserved in this School, and that the Academy will never have a deficit of pedagogues, just as there has never been a deficit of students. And as long as the School is alive, ballet will live on as we today understand it: as an art.

Conclusion

A ballerina of the Imperial ballet. A pedagogue of classical dance in the Soviet ballet school. The founder of a new, modern method of dance skills. The author of the first book on the science of classical dance. The first professor of choreography. People's Artist of the RSFSR. Laureate of the State Award of the USSR. A wise theorist, a great practitioner of ballet teaching. Counselor to many generations of talented ballerinas of Soviet ballet theater.

The life of Agrippina Yakovlevna ended abruptly, but the creation of her method of classical dance, convincing evidence of commitment and creative necessity, continued its path into art.

The generations of dancers change, but Vaganova's participation lives in each of them. It lives in those who today, on the 100th anniversary of her birth, dance on stage. And it will live 100 years after the death of this orthodox master of choreography.[1]

Agrippina Vaganova was a pioneer. She developed and codified a system of ballet training that became the standard against which many great dancers are judged. In Russia, nearly everyone holds the Vaganova Academy and its style in great reverence; the pedagogues and dancers mentioned on these pages serve Vaganova's legacy in their daily work in the studio and on stage.

As Vaganova's contemporary Fyodor Lopukhov wrote, "I don't doubt that classical dance of the twentieth century can overcome everything. But it is not necessary to confuse this with archaic form. Classical dance is constantly developing, both by its own rules and under the influence of other art forms. . . . I'm completely convinced that all the talented dancers of the future will surpass those that currently exist. The law of development consists of this."[2]

Indeed, the present has surpassed what preceded it. Legs are higher; technique is more refined; bravura steps are more numerous and delivered in greater quantity. We have *developpés* at 180 degrees, sixty-four *fouettés* instead of thirty-two. . . . But is that a sign of development, necessarily?

Technique, certainly, has progressed; Vaganova's system has lasted, in part, by evolving to meet new artistic needs. Just as Agrippina Yakovlevna herself adjusted her approach to steps in developing her method, so that technique has adapted to the changing times. The graduates of the Vaganova Academy today are different from their predecessors—longer, leaner, with higher extensions, more turns—but they stem from the same traditions. The precision in their technique, the uniformity of their corps de ballet, the consistent, shared basis for training are just some of the hallmarks of Vaganova's system. Harbingers of the "old school style" continue to teach and coach inside the theater, raising the younger generation, the more talented of whom have absorbed the best of past tradition, the basis of that technique, but also the ability to project emotion and soul, to inhabit a role or character on stage. The pedagogical system that formed over centuries now continues, still passed down to each generation "from hand to hand, from foot to foot." The Vaganova system itself remains highly insular, but not impenetrable by Western trends and influences.

The disagreements over the current state of Vaganova's style as discussed by today's Mariinsky and Vaganova Academy pedagogue-coaches underscore the importance of this school in the world of ballet and the great concern for it among those who continue to carry Vaganova's torch. Some think the tradition is disappearing or unnecessarily altered; others insist it is adapting and evolving as the great pedagogue herself intended. And some observe the preservation of the basic technical foundation of Vaganova's system at the expense of soulful, emotional expression. One could argue that exposure to Western influence has tarnished parts of what was a carefully preserved tradition during the Soviet years. Or that the passage of time and the evolution of the spectator's preferences have affected how this tradition is now viewed. Gabriela Komleva notes the shift in the ballet-going audience over the years.

> Earlier, there were more theater lovers, more fans. Since perestroika there has been a shift in the country, and there aren't enough resources for balletomanes because the pensioners cannot pay for expensive tickets. There are many reasons that now prevent people who are true balletomanes from attending performances. Meanwhile, the new viewers are not always dedicated—you have to love it and be dedicated. Ballet isn't pop culture, after all; it is an art of the chosen few, a selected elite, for those who understand it; and it is also an art that you have to learn and study.[3]

Unfortunately, today such study and awareness in the viewer has perhaps diminished somewhat over time, as ballet now competes with the developments and distractions of the twenty-first century.

Ballet, along with life in Russia, has evolved since Vaganova's day. Recognizing that tendency, Vaganova discouraged approaching her system as dogma, and encouraged the further development of ballet after her death. To a great extent, her method has in fact developed; and it has withstood the test of time. Ballet in Russia as whole has evolved, but to echo the many pedagogues' voices recorded on these pages, its core must continue to be preserved to avoid losing the classical base and foundation from which it has grown.

As Tatiana Terekhova pointed out, "When you spend a few years abroad and come back and you understand, 'Thank God, here [in Russia] there is still something to look at.'" That is perhaps the key to this entire puzzle. Indeed, each summer hundreds of tourists flock to the Mariinsky Ballet in its home theater and leave amazed, with lasting impressions of its dancers' deep artistry, dramatic expression, and high-level technique that is, in many minds, unparalleled anywhere else. Certainly the Russians are known for their incomparable talent in ballet; the Kirov-Mariinsky still exemplifies that worldwide. To hear these pedagogues speaking critically about their tradition is to recognize one crucial point: their argument exists on a plane several steps removed from the rest of the world, a plane where standards are higher, traditions deeper, and the pool of talent carefully selected and finely honed toward its ultimate success—a group of elite dancers that in some cases have no equals.

When the curtain goes up on the Mariinsky Ballet today, there is no doubt that this is a company that continues to be the epitome of refined, uniform classical ballet technique with deep historical traditions. Those traditions and that classical technique exist in great part thanks to the system founded by Agrippina Vaganova.

Vaganova's system endures, which speaks to its strength, longevity, and the heavy weight of tradition that it now carries, a tradition that has been supported by the Russian government, by social philanthropists, and by countless pedagogues and dancers who perpetuate it by devoting their life work to the art of ballet. If, as so many pedagogues insist, the core principles of Vaganova technique can continue to be preserved while adapting to the changing times, then Vaganova's system of ballet training will withstand any future vagaries that may arise in ballet, and will persist for decades to come.

More than one individual interviewed for this book referred to the Vaganova Academy as a hallowed place. Walking through either the Academy or the Mariinsky Theatre, one can feel the weight of tradition hanging heavy in the musty air. The twisting corridors and expansive studios of the Mariinsky Theatre and the long pristine hallways inside the Vaganova Academy are home to the heart and soul of Agrippina Yakovlevna's life work. For generations of pedagogues and dancers, both those just beginning their journey in ballet, and those who have already spent a lifetime in this world of toil, perseverance, and beauty, these institutions remain sanctuaries for a unique and time-tested form of art, that of classical ballet.

Notes

Introduction

1. Vaganova, *Osnovye*, 5.
2. Ibid.
3. Ibid., 9.

Chapter 1. Vaganova the Dancer

1. Blok, "Agrippina Yakovlevna," 36.
2. Ibid. Blok's description of summer training also comes from her article "Agrippina Yakovlevna," 36.
3. Slonimskiĭ, "Professor Klassicheskoga Tantsa," 9–10.
4. Vserossiskogo Teatralnogo Obshestvo (hereafter cited as VTO) *Vaganova—Stat'i Vspominanie Materialy*, 37.
5. Ibid.
6. Amirgamzaev, *Samye Znamenitye Mastera*, 33.
7. VTO, *Vaganova—Stat'i Vspominanie Materialy*, 38.
8. Ibid., 39.
9. Amirgamzaev, *Samye Znamenitye Mastera*, 38.
10. Blok, "Agrippina Yakovlevna," 36.
11. Vaganova, *Osnovye*, 6. The literal translation of the title of Vaganova's textbook is *Basic Principles of Classical Dance*, but the published title in English is *Basic Principles of Classical Ballet*.
12. Vasilieva, *Sekret Tantsa*, 182.
13. Oboĭmina and Tat'kova, *Yabloko Protianutoe Eve*, 204.
14. Blok, "Agrippina Yakovlevna," 36.
15. Vasilieva, *Sekret Tantsa*, 182.
16. Kremshevskaya, "Grammatika Agrippinoi Vaganovoi," 38.
17. Dolgopolov, *Minuvshikh Dnei Vspominanie*, 150.

18. Tikanova, *Devushka v Sinem*, 62.

19. Ibid., 79. "Plastique," refers to harmonious, graceful movement; a musical counterpart might be the sense of legato.

20. Pomina, "Vstrecha," 53.

21. Nijinska and Rawlinson, *Early Memoirs*, 116.

22. Kostrovitskaya, "Nachalo Sovetskoi Shkoli," 12.

23. Pomina, "Vstrecha," 53.

24. Zorich, "Fragmenti Avtobiografii," 43.

25. Fyodorchenko, "Olga Preobrazhenskaia," 80.

26. Messerer, *Tanets. Mysl. Vremya*, 135.

27. Duncan, *Isadora: Touring in Russia*, 92–93.

28. Tikanova, *Devushka v Sinem*, 72.

29. Ibid., 79.

30. Fyodorchenko, "Olga Preobrazhenskaia," 86.

31. Dolgopolov, *Minuvshikh Dnei*, 150.

32. Krasovskaya, *Agrippina Yakovlevna*, 28. *Plastika* (noun) or *plasticheski* (adjective) in Russian are terms taken from the French "plastique," which refers to harmonious, graceful movement; a musical counterpart might be the sense of legato.

33. Blok, "Agrippina Yakovlevna," 36.

34. Ibid.

35. Krasovskaya, *Vaganova—A Dance Journey*, 40.

36. Kremshevskaya, "Grammatika Agrippinoi Vaganovoi," 18–19.

37. Gaevskiĭ, "Diana i Acteon," 61.

38. Blok, "Urok Vaganova," *Klassicheskiĭ Tanets*, 338.

39. Ibid., 342.

40. Krasovskaya, "Dve Zhizni Vaganovoi," no. 10, 59.

41. Vasilieva, *Sekret Tantsa*, 182.

42. Kremshevskaya, *Agrippina Vaganova*, 20.

43. Amirgamzaeva, *Samye Znamenitye Mastera*, 38.

44. Blok, "Agrippina Yakovlevna," 36.

45. Ibid.

46. Ibid.

47. Ibid.

48. VTO, *Vaganova—Stat'i Vspominanie Materialy*, 47–49.

49. Blok, "Urok Vaganova," *Klassicheskiĭ Tanets*, 339.

50. Ibid., 339.

51. Kremshevskaya, *Agrippina Vaganova*, 15.

52. Lopukhov, *Khoreograficheskye Otkroivennosti*, 169.

53. Ibid., 172.

54. Krasovskaya, "Legat i Kazannaya Tsena," 95.

55. Tikanova, *Devushka v Sinem*, 109.

56. Blok, "Urok Vaganova," *Klassicheskiĭ Tanets*, 336.

57. Ibid., 339.

58. Lopukhov, *Khoreograficheskye Otkroivennosti*, 172.

59. Volinskiĭ, *Stat'i o Balete*, 177.

60. Blok, "Agrippina Vaganova," *Rabochiĭ i Teatr*, 38.

61. Shelest, "Akademia Tantsa," 39.

62. Vaganova, *Osnovye*, 4.

63. Volinksiĭ, "Proshalnogo Benefisa Vaganovoi," in *Stat'i o Balete*, 177–80.

64. Slonimskiĭ, "Professor Klassicheskoga Tantsa," 9.

65. Ibid.

66. Lopukhov, *Khoreograficheskye Otkroivennosti*, 182.

67. Amirgamzaeva, *Samye Znamenitye Mastera*, 42.

68. Gaevskiĭ, "Vaganova Segodnia," 129.

69. VTO, *Vaganova—Stat'i Vspominanie Materialy*, 172.

70. Ibid., 60.

Chapter 2. Vaganova the Teacher

1. Kostrovitskaya, "Nachalo Sovetskoi Shkoli," 26.

2. Vaganova, *Osnovye*, 8.

3. Sergeyev, "K 100 Letiu," 26.

4. VTO, *Vaganova—Stat'i Vspominanie Materialy*, 58.

5. Kremshevskaya, "Grammatika Agrippinoi Vaganovoi," 41.

6. Ibid., 40.

7. VTO, *Vaganova—Stat'i Vspominanie Materialy*, 9.

8. Slonimskiĭ, "Professor Klassicheskoga Tantsa," 9.

9. VTO, *Vaganova—Stat'i Vspominanie Materialy*, 9.

10. Kremshevskaya, "Grammatika Agrippinoi Vaganovoi," 18–19.

11. Vaganova, *Osnovye*, 5–6.

12. Ibid., 8.

13. Gaevskiĭ, "Diana i Akteon," 59.

14. Tikanova, *Devushka v Sinem*, 62.

15. Fyodorchenko, "Olga Preobrazhenskaia," 80.

16. Vaganova, *Osnovye*, 8

17. Ibid.

18. Ibid.

19. Ibid.

20. Shelest, "Dialektika Pedagogika," 29.

21. Vaganova, *Osnovye*, 5.

22. Semënova, "K 100 Letiu," 28.

23. Blok, "Agrippina Yakovlevna," 38.

24. Ibid.

25. Blok, "Urok Vaganova," *Klassicheskiĭ Tanets*, 441.
26. VTO, *Vaganova—Stat'i Vspominanie Materialy*, 10.
27. Blok, "Agrippina Yakovlevna," 38.
28. VTO, *Vaganova—Stat'i Vspominanie Materialy*, 257.
29. Sergeyev, "K 100 Letiu," 26.
30. Blok, "Urok Vaganova," *Klassicheskiĭ Tanets*, 338.
31. Lopukhov, *Khoreograficheskye Otkroivennosti*, 172.
32. Ibid., 180. Emphases my own.
33. Evment'ieva, *Zapiski Ballerinoi*, 57.
34. VTO, *Vaganova—Stat'i Vspominanie Materialy*, 64.
35. Gaevskiĭ, *Dom Petipa*, 230–31.
36. Souritz, *Soviet Choreographers*, 72.
37. Ibid., 152.
38. Ibid., 240, 250.
39. Ibid., 279.
40. Ibid., 280.
41. Ibid., 277.
42. Gaevskiĭ, "Diana i Akteon," 60.
43. VTO, *Vaganova—Stat'i Vspominanie Materialy*, 262.
44. Lopukhov, *Writings on Ballet*, 155.
45. Ibid., 156.
46. VTO, *Vaganova—Stat'i Vspominanie Materialy*, 66.
47. Ibid., 199.
48. Ibid., 262–63.
49. Ibid., 88. Emphasis my own.
50. Krasovskaya, *Vaganova—A Dance Journey*, 149.
51. Ibid., 156.
52. Lopukhov, *Writings on Ballet*, 160.
53. Slonimskiĭ, *The Soviet Ballet*, 64.
54. Blok, "Urok Vaganova," *Klassicheskiĭ Tanets*, 339.
55. Sergeyev, "K 100 Letiu," 26–29.
56. Ibid.
57. Leontieva, Gerdt, and Lukom, "Shto Delat C Baletom?" 31.
58. Sergeyev, "K 100 Letiu," 26.
59. Amirgamzaev, *Samye Znamenitye Mastera*, 48.
60. VTO, *Vaganova—Stat'i Vspominanie Materialy*, 70.
61. Krasovskaya, *Vaganova—A Dance Journey*, 170.
62. Ibid., 171.
63. Evment'ieva, *Zapiski Balerinoi*, 60.
64. Dudinskaya, "Ob Agrippinoi Yakovlevnoi Vaganovoi," 26–30.
65. Krasovskaya, *Vaganova—A Dance Journey*, 179.

66. Shelest, "Akademia Tantsa," 39–41.

67. Trofimova, interview, July 10, 2009.

68. Souritz, *Bolshaia Rossisskaia Entsiklopedia*, 811.

69. VTO, *Vaganova—Stat'i Vspominanie Materialy*, 63.

70. Ibid., 80.

71. Souritz, *Bolshaia Rossisskaia Entsiklopedia*, 811.

72. Krasovskaya, *Vaganova—A Dance Journey*, 189.

73. VTO, *Vaganova—Stat'i Vspominanie Materialy*, 77.

74. Krasovskaya, "Dve Zhizni Vaganovoi," no. 10, 60.

75. Krasovskaya, *Vaganova—A Dance Journey*, 195.

76. Evment'ieva, *Zapiski Balerinoi*, 60.

77. Lopukhov, *Writings on Ballet*, 167.

78. Krasovskaya, *Vaganova—A Dance Journey*, 193.

79. Ibid., 199.

80. Sergeyev, "K 100 Letiu," 26–29.

81. Krasovskaya, "Dve Zhizni Vaganovoi," no. 10, 66.

82. VTO, *Vaganova—Stat'i Vspominanie Materialy*, 77.

83. Ibid., 70.

84. Blok, "Urok Vaganova," *Klassicheskiĭ Tanets*, 338.

85. Dudinskaya, "Ob Agrippinoi Yakovlevnoi Vaganovoi," 26–30.

86. Shelest, "Akademia Tantsa," 29.

87. Ibid., 39.

88. Kremshevskaya, "Grammatika Agrippinoi Vaganovoi," 18.

89. Ibid.

90. Mikhailov, *Molodye Godi*, 19.

91. Semënova, "K 100 Letiu," 28.

92. Kremshevskaya, "Grammatika Agrippinoi Vaganovoi," 19.

93. VTO, *Vaganova—Stat'i Vspominanie Materialy*, 172.

94. Osipenko, interview, July 15, 2009.

95. Abdulkhakova and Shatilov, "Ne Kazhdiĭ Artist," 6.

96. Kremshevskaya, "Grammatika Agrippinoi Vaganovoi," 19.

97. Ibid.

98. Ibid.

99. Ibid.

Chapter 3. Vaganova Today: Her Students

1. Adeyeva, "Pedagogika Klassicheskogo Tantsa," 123.

2. Kekisheva, interview, April 5, 2009.

3. Abdulkhakova and Shatilov, "Ne Kazhdiĭ Artist," 6. Shatilov's last sentence underlines the point that, when running on stage, dancers are not meant to look like pedestrians; noticeable bent knees are not the desired look.

4. Adeyeva, "Pedagogika Klassicheskogo Tantsa," 124. Other observations from Adeyeva are also from this article.

5. Komleva, interview, April 9, 2009.

6. Terekhova, interview, April 20, 2009.

7. Kurgapkina, interview, April 15, 2009.

8. Sergeyev, "K 100 Letiu," 26–29. Tatiana Vecheslova quotes Vaganova.

9. Abdulkhakova and Shatilov, "Ne Kazhdiĭ Artist," 7.

10. Vecheslova, *O Tom, Shto Dorogo*, 132.

11. Ibid., 133.

12. Komleva, "Reperatuar Shkoli," 116.

13. Vaganova, *Osnovye*, 47.

14. Ibid., 67.

15. Ibid., 37.

16. Naidich and Pomerantseva. "Priglasheniia," 15.

17. Lopukhov, *Khoreograficheskye Otkroivennosti*, 161.

18. Duprati et al., "A Dance to the Music," http://www.plosone.org/article/info%3Adoi%2F10.1371%2Fjournal.pone.0005023.

19. Seliutskiĭ, interviews, April 15 and July 18, 2009.

20. Shelest, "Akademia Tantsa," 40.

21. The Vaganova Academy's grading system correlates with the Russian academic system, in which marks are given from 1–5, 5 being the best—somewhat equivalent to the Western grading system of A to F.

22. Oleinik and Dudinskaya, 19.

23. Lopukhov, *Khoreograficheskye Otkroivennosti*, 152.

24. Chistiakova, interviews, November 2007 and July 2009.

25. Gaevskiĭ, *Dom Petipa*, 372.

26. Ibid., 371–72.

27. Ibid., 372.

28. Ibid, 376.

29. Lopatkina, interview, July 22, 2009.

30. Kremshevskaya, *Agrippina Vaganova*, 91.

31. VTO, *Vaganova—Stat'i Vspominanie Materialy*, 190.

32. Vikulov, interview, July 18, 2009.

33. Fokine, *Protiv Techenie*, 437. This excerpt was first published in *Novoe Russkoe Slovo* [New Russian Word] in 1935, on April 14. I used the Russian version of Fokine's *Protiv* as the basis for my translation.

34. Kostrovitskaya, "Nachalo Sovetskoi Shkoli," 27–28.

35. Abdulkhakova and Shatilov. "Ne Kazhdiĭ Artist," 7.

36. Sergeyev, "K 100 Letiu," 26.

37. Vaganova, *Osnovye*, xiii.

38. Asylmuratova, "Metodika Vaganovoi," 59–73.

Conclusion

1. Kremshevskaya, "Grammatika Agrippinoi Vaganovoi," 19.
2. Lopukhov, *Khoreograficheskye Otkroivennosti*, 24.
3. Komleva, interview, April 9, 2009.

Bibliography

Abdulkhakova, Rimma with Konstantin Shatilov. "Ne Kazhdiĭ Artist Mozhet Byt Pedagogom." [Not Every Artist Can Be a Pedagogue] *Linia* no. 4 *(supplement to "Balet" magazine)* (April 2004): 6–7.

Adeyeva, Larisa Mikhailovna. "Pedagogika Klassicheskogo Tantsa—Kharakteristika Professii." [The Pedagogy of Classical Dance—Characteristics of the Profession] *Khoreograficheskoe Isskustvo*. St. Petersburg: Kirov, 2007.

Akademicheskoe Gosudarstvennaya Khoreograficheskoe Uchilishe Imeni Vaganovoi. [The Vaganova Academic State Choreographic School] Leningrad: Muzika, 1988.

Alovert, Nina. "Naslednitsi Vaganovoi." [Vaganova's Heiresses] *Balet* no. 3 (May 2005): 47.

Amirgamzaev, Olga. *Samye Znamenitye Mastera Baleta Rossiia*. [The Most Famous Masters of Russian Ballet] Moscow: Veche, 2002.⁰

Asylmuratova, Altynai. "Metodika Vaganovoi." [The Vaganova Method] *Vestnik ARB* no. 9 (2001): 59–73.

Avdish, David. "Mysli Vslukh." [Thinking Aloud] *Ballet ad Libatum* no. 4. (2008): 30–31.

Baletmeister Marius Petipa—Stat'i, Issledovanie, Razmyshleniia. [Balletmaster Marius Petipa—Articles, Research, Reflections] Vladimir: Foliant, 2006.

Baranova, Irina. *Irina—Ballet, Life and Love*. Gainesville: University Press of Florida, 2005.

Belikova, Elena. "Tsekh: Goriachi Dni." [TSEKh: Hot Days] *Balet* no. 1 (2004): 38–39.

"Biograficheskaia Spravka—Marius Petipa i Russkaia Khoreografiia." [Biographical Information—Marius Petipa and Russian Choreography] *Za Sovetskoe Iskusstvo* no. 10 (May 1947).

Blok, Ludmila. "Agrippina Yakovlevna." *Rabochiĭ i Teatr* (1937): 36–38.

———. "Urok Vaganova." [Vaganova Lesson] *Klassicheskiĭ Tanets—Istoriia i Sovremennosti*. Moscow: Iskusstvo, 1987.

"Chestvovanie Olgi Osipovnoi Preobrazhenskoi." [Celebration of Olga Osipovna Preobrajenska] *Obozrenie Teatrov* (1909): 907–949.

Chul, Zhanna. *V Plenu u Terpsikhora*. [Taken Prisoner by Terpsichore] St. Petersburg: Pirouette Publishers, 1997.

Dolgopolov, Mikhail. *Minuvshikh Dnei Vspominanie*. [Remembrance of Days Gone By] Leningrad: Izvestia, 1997.

Dudinskaya, Natalia. "Ob Agrippinoi Yakovlevnoi Vaganovoi." [About Agrippina Yakovlevna Vaganova] *Teatr* no. 6 (1983): 26–30.

Duncan, Isadora. "Isadora: Touring Russia." Moscow: Artist. Regisseur. Teatr., 1992.

Duprati, Elena, Marco Iosa, and Patrick Haggard. "A Dance to the Music of Time: Aesthetically-Relevant Changes in Body Posture in Performing Art." University of Cambridge (March 26, 2009), http://www.plosone.org/article/info%3Adoi%2 F10.1371%2Fjournal.pone.0005023

Entsiklopedicheskiĭ Slovar.' [Encyclopedic Dictionary] St. Petersburg: I. A. Efron and F. A. Brokghaus, 1898.

Evment'ieva, Lidia Vasilievna. *Zapiski Balerinoi.* [Recordings of a Ballerina] Leningrad: 1931. (Published at the author's own expense).

Fedorenko, Elena. "Puti Emplua: Benefis Uliani Lopatkinoi v Moskve." [The Path of Emploi: Uliana Lopatkina's Gala in Moscow] *Kultura* no. 5 (2008): 10.

Fokine, Mikhail. *Protiv Techenie—Vspominanie Baletmastera—Stat'i i Pisma*. [Against the Tide—Remembrances of a Balletmaster—Articles and Letters] Leningrad/ Moscow: "Art" Publishers, 1962.

Frangopulo, Marietta. *Agrippina Yakovlevna Vaganova—50 Let Raboti v Balete.* [Agrippina Yakovlevna Vaganova—50 Years of Work in Ballet] Leningrad: BTO (VTO): The Leningrad Branch of All Russian Theatrical Society of the Leningrad State Museum, 1948.

Fyodorchenko, Oleg. "Olga Preobrazhenskaia, Pedagog Petersburgskogo Teatralnogo Uchilishe." [Olga Preobrajenska, Pedagogue of the Petersburg Theatre School] *Vestnik ARB* no. 5 (1995): 80.

Gaevskiĭ, Vadim. "Diana i Akteon, ili klass Vaganovoi v 20x–30x." [Diana and Acteon, or Vaganova's Class in the '20s and '30s] *Moskovskiĭ Nabliudatel'* no. 1 (1993): 58–65.

———. *Dom Petipa*. Moscow: Artist. Regisseur. Teatr., 2000.

———. "Vaganova Segodnia." [Vaganova Today] *Teatr* no. 4 (2002): 127–129.

Gennadiĭ Nayumovich Seliutskiĭ—K Yubileiu Baletmaster-Repetitora, Zasluzhenogo Deiatelia Iskusstv Rossii, Professora [Gennadi Naumovich Seliutskiĭ—The Anniversary of the Balletmaster-Repetiteur, Honored Arts Worker of Russia, and Professor] St. Petersburg: Avrora-Design, 2007.

Gubskaya, Irina. "Pedagogicheskaia Legenda—Mariinskiĭ Teatr Ustroil Tvorcheskiĭ Vecher Gennadiya Selutskogo." [Pedagogical Legend—The Mariinsky Theatre Held an Artistic Evening for Gennadi Seliutskiĭ] *Kultura* no. 19 (May 2007): 12.

Komleva, Gabriela. "Reperatuar Shkoli." [Repertoire of the School] *Vestnik ARB* no. 9 (2001): 116.

Kostrovitskaya, Vera. "Nachalo Sovetskoi Shkoli Klassicheskoga Tantsa." [The Beginning of the Soviet School of Classical Dance] *Mastera Baleta—Samodeiatelnosti. Metodicheskye Posobie*. Moscow: Iskusstvo, 1978.

Krasovskaya, Vera. "Agrippina Yakovlevna Vaganova." Leningrad: Agraph Publishers, 1999, p. 28.

———. "Dve Zhizni Vaganovoi, Ballet Povest." [Two Lives of Vaganova, a Ballet Tale] NEVA no. 9 (1985): 75–103.

———. "Dve Zhizni Vaganovoi, Ballet Povest." [Two Lives of Vaganova, a Ballet Tale] NEVA no. 10 (1985): 26–76.

———. "Legat i Kazannaya Tsena." ["Legat and the Official Stage"] Russkiï Baletno-go Teatra Nachalo XX Veka. Leningrad: Planeta Muziki, 1971.

———. Vaganova—A Dance Journey from Petersburg to Leningrad. Gainesville: University Press of Florida, 2005.

———. "Vspominanie Agrippinoi Yakovlevnoi Vaganovoi." [Recollections of Agrippina Yakovlevna Vaganova] Literaturnaia Gazeta no. 24 (2000): 8.

Kremshevskaya, Galina. "Grammatika Agrippinoi Vaganovoi." [The Grammar of Agrippina Vaganova] Muzikal'naia Zhizn' no. 13 (1979): 18–19.

———. Agrippina Vaganova. Leningrad: Iskusstvo, 1981.

"K 100 Letiu Co Dnya Rozhdeniia Agrippinoi Yakovlevnoi Vaganovoi." [On the 100th Anniversary of Agrippina Yakovlevna Vaganova's Birthday] Teatralnaia Zhizn' no. 11 (1979): 26–30.

Leningradskiï Balet Segodnia. [Leningrad Ballet Today] Moscow: Iskusstvo, 1968.

Leontieva, L., Elizaveta Gerdt, and E. Lukom. "Shto Delat C Baletom?" [What Is to Be Done about Ballet?] Zhizhn' Iskusstva no. 7 (17 Feb.): 31.

Levinson, Andrei. "Voznesennaya Magiei Iskusstva." [The Rising Magic of Art] Sovremennii Balet no. 1 (1991): 38–40.

Lopukhov, Fyodor. Khoreograficheskye Otkroivennosti. [Choreographic Openness] Leningrad: Isskustvo, 1937.

———. Writings on Ballet and Music. Madison: University of Wisconsin Press, 2002.

M. I. Petipa 1822–1922 K Stoletiu co Dnia Rozhdeniia. [M. I. Petipa 1822–1922 The 100th Anniversary of His Birthday] St. Petersburg: R.V. Ts. Petrograd, 1922.

Marius Petipa—Materialy Vspominaniia Stat'i [Marius Petipa—Materials Recollections Articles] Edited by L. Filatova. Leningrad: Iskusstvo, 1971.

Marius Petipa. Compiled by A. Ignatenko. St. Petersburg: Soyuz Khudozhnikov, 2003.

Messerer, Asaf. Tanets. Mysl. Vremya. [Dance. Thought. Time.] Moscow: Isskystvo, 1990.

Mikhailov, Mikhail. Molodye Godi Leningradskogo Baleta. [Early Years of the Leningrad Ballet] Leningrad: Iskusstvo, 1978.

Naidich, Iuriï and M. A. Pomerantseva. "Priglasheniia K Razmyshleniu." [Invitation to Reflection] Vestnik ARB no. 10 (2002): 11–31.

Nijinska, Bronislava. Ranee Vspominanie. [Early Memoirs] Moscow: Artist. Regisseur. Teatr., 1999.

Nijinska, Bronislava. Early Memoirs. Translated and edited by Irina Nijinska and Jean Rawlinson. New York: Holt, Rinehart and Winston, 1981.

"Ninella Alexandrovna Kurgapkina." *Kultura* no. 8 (14–20 May, 2009): 2.

"Nuzhno Govorit." [It's Necessary to Talk] *Vestnik ARB* no. 17, 2007 // Ballet ad Libitum no. 4.

Oboïmina, Elena and Ol'ga Tat'kova. *Yabloko Protianutoe Eve*. [The Apple Bitten by Eve] Moscow: ACT, 2005.

Oleinik, Tat'iana, with Natalia Dudinskaya. "Ya Za Effekt v Balete." [I'm for Effects/Tricks in Ballet] *Teatralnaia Zhizn'* no. 16. (1988): 19.

Oxford Dictionary of Dance. Oxford: Oxford University Press, 2005.

Pavis, Patrice. "Emploi." *The Theatre Dictionary*. Moscow: GITIS Press: 2003.

Pogodin, N., ed. "Teatralnii Dnevnik: Molodëzh Leningradskogo Baleta." [Theatrical Diary: The Youth of Leningrad Ballet] *Teatr* no. 5 (1953): 104.

Pomina, Vera. "Vstrecha c Olgoi Preobrazhenskoi." [Meeting with Olga Preobrajenska] *Sovremennii Balet* no. 6 (1983): 53–54.

Preobrazhenskaya, Olga Osipovna. "Vyskazivanie Balerina ob Arte Isadora Duncan." [The Ballerina's Views on the Art of Isadora Duncan] *Teatr* [First published 1908] Leningrad: ART Publishers, 1992.

Rukhlya, Svetlana. "I Ispanskaya Krestyanka, i Feya Vesni." [A Spanish Peasant and a Spring Fairy] *Sankt Peterburg Vedomosti* no. 1 (Jan. 11, 2010): http://www.spbvedomosti.ru/print.htm?id=10263685@SV_Articles.

Russkii Balet: Bolshaia Russkaia Entsiklopedia. Moscow: Izdatelstvo Soglasiye, 1997.

Semënova, Marina. "K 100 Letiu Co Dnya Rozhdeniia Agrippini Yakovlevnoi Vaganovoi." [The 100th Anniversary of Agrippina Yakovlevna Vaganova's Birthday] *Teatralnaia Zhizn'* no. 11 (1979): 28.

Sergeyev, Konstantin. "K 100 Letiu Co Dnya Rozhdeniia Agrippini Yakovlevnoi Vaganovoi." [The 100th Anniversary of Agrippina Yakovlevna Vaganova's Birthday] *Teatralnaia Zhizn'* no. 11 (1979): 26–29.

Shelest, Alla. "Akademia Tantsa." [Academy of Dance] *Sovremennii Balet* no. 5 (1982): 39–41.

———. "Dialektika Pedagogika." [Dialectics of Pedagogy] *Teatralnaia Zhizn'* no. 11 (1979): 29.

Shiriaev, Alexander. *Riadom c Petipa*. [Next to Petipa] Leningrad: VTO, 1938.

Slonimskiï, Iuriï. "Professor Klassicheskoga Tantsa." [Professor of Classical Dance] *Muzikal'naia Zhizn'* no. 24 (1961): 9–10.

———. *The Soviet Ballet*. New York: Philosophical Library, 1947.

Solerinskiï, I., ed. *Uchebnii Plan i Programy Vyistuplenikh, Ispitanye*. [Study Plan and Programs of Graduation, Training] Leningrad: Len Stat Khoregrafik Teknikum, 1928.

Souritz, Elizabeth, ed. *Bolshaia Rossisskaia Entsiklopedia*. Moscow: Rospechat, 1998.

Souritz, Elizabeth. *Soviet Choreographers in the 1920s*. Durham and London: Duke University Press: 1990.

Stupnikov, Igor and Arsen Degan. *Peterburgskiĭ Balet 1903–2003*. St. Petersburg: Baltic Seasons, 2003.

Svetlov, Valerian. *Sovremennĭ Balet*. [Modern Ballet] St. Petersburg: P. Tolike and A. Villeborge, 1911.

"Teatralnĭ Dnevnik: Molodëzh Leningradskogo Baleta." *Teatr* no. 5 (1953): 104.

Tikanova (Tikhonova), Nina. *Devushka v Sinem*. [The Girl in Blue] Leningrad: Art Publishers, 1982.

Tri Veka Sankt Peterburga—Entsiklopedia Dvadsatogo Veka. [Three Centuries of Saint Petersburg—Encyclopedia of the Twentieth Century] St. Petersburg: Philological Department of Saint Petersburg State University, 2006. Volume II.

Tsai, Nadezhda. "Ritsar Tantsa." [Knight of Dance] *Linia* no. 4 (April 2006): 6.

Vaganova, Agrippina. *Osnovye Klassicheskogo Tantsa*. [Basic Principles of Classical Dance, Russian edition] Moscow: Art Publishers, 1963.

Vasilieva, Tatiana. *Sekret Tantsa*. [Secret of Dance] St. Petersburg: Diamant Zolotoi Vek, 1997.

Vecheslova, Tatiana. *O Tom, Shto Dorogo*. [About That Which Is Valuable] Leningrad: Sovetsky Kompozitor, 1984.

Volinskiĭ, Akim. *Stat'i o Balete*. [Articles about Ballet] SPB: Hyperion Press, 2002.

———. *Kniga Likovanye*. [Book of Triumphs] Moscow: Art Publishers, 1992.

Vserossiskogo Teatralnogo Obshestvo, Leningradskiĭ Otdel. *Agrippina Yakovlevna Vaganova—Stat'i Vspominanie Materialy*. [Agrippina Yakovlevna Vaganova—Articles Recollections Materials] Leningrad: Iskusstvo, 1958.

Vyrubova, Nina. "Moi Russkiĭ Uchitel.'" [My Russian Teacher] *Moskovskiĭ Nabliudatel'* no. 1 (1993): 55–57.

Yakubova, Irina. "Tatiana Terekhova." *Mariinskiĭ Teatr* no. 5 (1994): 8.

Zakharov, Rostislav. *Socheneniya Tantsa—Stranitsye Pedagogicheskikh Opitov*. [Compositions of Dance—Pages of Pedagogical Experience] Moscow: Iskusstvo, 1989.

Zorich, Iuriĭ. "Fragmenti Avtobiografii." [Fragments of an Autobiography] *Balet* no. 1 (1995): 43.

Zozulina, Natalia. *Alla Osipenko*. Leningrad: Iskusstvo, 1987.

Index

Chart of Transliterated Terms

Russian	Library of Congress	Transliteration Americanization/ Use in This Book
Кшесинская	Kshessinskaya	Kshesinska
Преображенская	Preobrazhenskaya	Preobrajenska
Сергеев	Sergeyev	
Фокин	Fokin	Fokine
Константин	Konstantin	Konstantin
Дудинская	Dudinskaia	Dudinskaya

Page numbers in italics refer to illustrations.

Adeyeva, Ludmila, 79
Anisimov, Nikolai, 65
Asylmuratova, Altynai, 166, *168, 169, 170, 171*; on pedagogues at Academy, 173; published article in *Vestnik*, 171; reevaluating Academy program, 174; and Vaganova's style over time, 172
Audiences, in Russia, 132–34, 181

Balanchine, George, 23, 128, *129*, 132
Baltflot, 11, 30
Bayadère, La, 16; Chistiakova comments on, 142; Terekhova in, 122; Vaganova in, 20
Bazarova, Nadezhda, 72
Blok, Ludmila: on ballets in Vaganova's reper-toire, 10; comparing French and Italian styles, 10; comparing Vaganova to Pavlova, 25; and Fokine influence, 33; on Kshesinska, 20–21; on N. Legat training method, 20, 23; quoting N. Legat, 23; review of Vaganova's dancing in *Petersburg Page,* 20; review of Vaganova in *Paquita,* 21; on Telyakovsky directorship, 20; on Vaganova adhering to French school, 17; Vaganova as director of theater, 50; on

Vaganova beginning her studies, 5–6; on Vaganova's admiration for Cecchetti, 10; on Vaganova's early retirement, 27; on Vaganova's graduation performance, 15–16; on Vaganova in *La Source,* 10; on Vaganova preserving students's individuality, 41; on Vaganova's structured lesson plans, 36–38; on Vaganova's teaching/lessons, 39
Bolt, 49
Bronze Horseman, The, *127,* 129

Cecchetti, Enrico, 9–10; fixed lesson plans, 36
Chistiakova, Irina, 134, *136, 137, 153*; on children pursuing ballet, 147; on dramatic expression, 144, 148–49; on flexibility and gymnastics, 143, 150; on pedagogues, 143; on the role of Gamzat-ti, 142; on stage partnerships, 148; on teaching, 142–44; on theater politics, 143, 146; on theater work, 140–41; training and graduation, 137–39; in Varna Competition, 139–40
Chopiniana, 23–25, 33, 77, 128
Cinderella, 125, 128, 139
Corsaire, Le, 92, 109, 122, 139–40

Catherine E. Pawlick began studying ballet at the age of six in the San Francisco Bay Area. She performed with regional ballet companies in both California and Washington, D.C. Following intensive Russian language training through a bachelor of science degree in languages and linguistics from Georgetown University, she began a new career as a ballet critic. She moved to St. Petersburg in 2004, where she remains a full-time resident.

Pawlick has written for the *San Francisco Chronicle*, the *Moscow Times*, *Ballet Review, Dance Magazine*, and CriticalDance.com. She has worked as correspondent for *Dance Europe* magazine (London) since 2005 and *Danza i Danza* (Italy) since 2017. More of her writing can be seen at http://VaganovaToday.com.

CPSIA information can be obtained
at www.ICGtesting.com
Printed in the USA
BVHW081937290822
645335BV00001B/97

9 780813 068718